Ottakars LOCAL HISTORY *Series*

Huddersfield

Market Place, Huddersfield, c. 1900.

Ottakars LOCAL HISTORY *Series*

Huddersfield

To Andrew
Best Wishes
Nik

Compiled by
Nik Taylor

TEMPUS

First published 2001
Copyright © Nik Taylor, 2001

Ottakar's Local History Series

Produced in association with
Tempus Publishing Limited
The Mill, Brimscombe Port,
Stroud, Gloucestershire, GL5 2QG

ISBN 0 7524 2283 9

Typesetting and origination by
Tempus Publishing Limited
Printed in Great Britain by
Midway Colour Print, Wiltshire

Acknowledgements

We would like to thank all those who helped in the making of the book, including John Boyd, Brian Haigh and BBC Radio Leeds who greatly helped in the early publicity for the competition. The same goes for Greg Pogson at the *Huddersfield Daily Examiner*. We would also like to thank the *Examiner's* photographic archive for their help.

Thanks also go to the Kirklees Library service and the Huddersfield University Library. Most of all thank you to everyone who entered the competition – it really shows history is alive and well and thriving in Huddersfield.

Contents

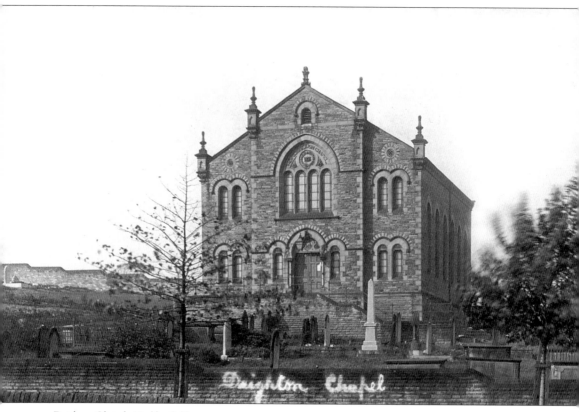

Deighton Chapel, Huddersfield.

Foreword

Local and family history have never been more popular; just take a look at the shelves of your favourite bookshop, or try to find a vacant seat in the Local Studies Library on a busy midweek afternoon.

Exhibitions which tell the stories of local people and places are amongst the most visited attractions in the museums which the Kirklees Community History Service manages. The Millennium encouraged many communities to mount their own exhibitions and we have been pleased to help and advise. The service supports a network of over thirty groups and organizations whose members are interested in local history and heritage matters.

Some of the groups are planning their own publications and we are assisting an increasing number of individuals to write about themes from the rich and varied history of the area and its people. Local and family historians have not been slow to recognize the benefits of the Internet for sharing and gathering information and, with a personal computer, everyone is a potential author.

I am delighted that so many writers have come forward to take part in this project. It is particularly gratifying that so many new writers have been given the opportunity to be contributors; I hope they are thrilled to see their first work in print. I am sure that the book will give pleasure to a great many readers who want to know more about the locality or indulge themselves in nostalgia.

As a regular contributor to John Boyd's Radio Leeds phone-in, *Who? What? Where?*, I know the value which people place on shared memories which evoke a bygone age. Stories of National Service, bath night in front of a blazing fire, or going 'mumming' on New Year's Eve mean nothing to today's young people. But for those generations born before the Second World War, they help to bring back happy days, sad times, old friends, forgotten events and familiar places.

Reminiscence can have a therapeutic value too. It can provide stimulation and comfort for older people. It may help some people recover short-term memory. It brings generations together and gives voice and value to older members of the community. The Community History Service has been instrumental in setting up the local Reminiscence Network which provides support, ideas and training for carers and others who work with older people. Memory Boxes containing audio tapes, photographs and objects from the past are the latest initiative to help trigger the memories of the elderly.

Local history is not just for older people. I was at junior school when I started asking the questions which gave me an interest which has lasted the whole of my life. You don't have to

The first Sunday school queen at Deighton Methodist church, 1933-1934. From left to right: Olwyn Marshall (attendant), Blanche Mellor (queen in waiting), Winifred Holmes (fourth attendant), Bessie Armitage (Queen), Rosie Garron (patient), Teresa Day (Mayor), Law Taylor. (Photograph supplied by Hazel wheeler.)

be at school either. In fact, you can come to local history at any age and from any background. Finding out about where we live is about putting down roots which is important in an age of constant change. Knowing about our town or village, its history and traditions and what makes it distinctive, helps to give us a sense of identity and a feeling of belonging.

I hope that *Ottakar's Local History Series* will encourage many more people to tell their stories, to undertake research and to set pen to paper, and I too look forward to finding more of their accounts of people, places and memories on the shelves of my favourite bookshop.

Brian Haigh, Tolson Museum,
Community History Manager, July, 2001

CHAPTER 1

People

Entrance to Crosland Lodge, now the Liberal club.

The Croslands of Crosland Moor

As a child, growing up in the Midlands, I was raised on tales and family stories of my Huddersfield ancestors and relatives; of Members of Parliament, grand houses and civic duty. On arriving in Huddersfield as an adult I discovered that there was little obvious evidence about my Crosland ancestors. The event that inspired me to want to document some of their contributions to the town, was a visit to Royds Mount (now Huddersfield Grammar School). My guide around the school said it had been the home of the Crowther family, but had no idea that it was a Crosland that built the house in the first place.

The legacy that the Croslands have left in Huddersfield comes in the shape of the many buildings, originally homes or warehouses, but now used for other purposes. These buildings are monuments and memorials to the work they pursued, their activities and their lives.

Early settlers

Thomas Crosland was one of the earliest settlers in the Crosland Moor area, which in the mid-eighteenth century was open moorland on the road between Huddersfield and Manchester. Thomas Crosland was a woollen manufacturer, as were many of his descendants. His sons used to carry pieces of woven cloth to market on their shoulders. At the same time the family acquired land in the area.

George Crosland (1789-1864)

It was George who expanded the family business by building Crosland Moor Mills, on Crosland Moor, with the first mill engines starting in 1832. In the 1851 Census there were 186 men and 150 women employed at the mill – a total workforce of 342 people. Over the years the company continued to expand and Crosland Moor Mill increased slightly in size. George Crosland retired in 1860, and was succeed in the business by his sons. The mill unfortunately burnt down in 1915, whilst busy manufacturing khaki and army clothing. At the time there were 400 workers in the mill.

George married three times; he had a son with his first wife, who died in childbirth. He had a further six children with his second wife.

Family home of George Crosland

As prosperity followed the building of the first mill, the family built *Crosland Lodge*, on land adjoining the mill. This building, which still stands, originally stood in four acres of land. The house was built in ashlar stone with an impressive entrance of six finely carved columns. It has been much altered over the years and is in need of renovation but the family crest can still be seen today above the entrance. The Lodge today is the Crosland Moor Liberal Club.

The Lodge itself cannot be seen from Blackmoorfoot Road but anyone who travels the road will be able to see the two Lodge Gatehouses; one at the crossroads with Park Road and the other lower down on the corner with Moorside Avenue. The land that originally formed the estate has been built on over the years, but the bowling green in front of the house, established in 1927, remains.

Not far from Crosland Lodge, along Park Road, is more evidence of Crosland settlement. At the entrance to Park Works (David Brown's) stand two pillars, which would have stood either side of the driveway up to the house known as Park Cottage (now demolished); the Crosland crests are carved on the two pillars. The top shield is the crest found at other family homes (Royds Wood), and on several graves in Edgerton Cemetery. The bottom elliptical crest is emblazoned on chinaware which has been passed down different branches of the family.

'The Crosland Army'

The family story was that the Croslands had had their own army, and that some chinaware still kept by the family had been used by the soldiers. In some ways it seemed a rather far fetched story but a *Northern Star* newspaper article of 4 April 1840 mentioned that: 'Mr George Crosland, of Crosland Moor, had received a large quantity of clothing, similar to military uniform, for the purpose of establishing a corps of volunteers to assist his party to obtain a repeal of the Corn Laws.' Maybe there is more than a grain of truth in this family tale?

The Britannia Building

When one arrives in Huddersfield by train, and emerges from the station into St George's Square, one would straight away see the impressive Britannia Building, built by George Crosland between 1856 and 1859. The Britannia Building was constructed as a warehouse for George Crosland; he used some of the rooms himself and let others so that the buyers did not have to travel out to the mills to see the pieces of fabrics. George Crosland bought the land for the warehouse from the Ramsden Estate; initially he offered 1s 3d per yard but the fixed price was 1s 6d per yard. The building now houses the offices of the Yorkshire Building Society.

The Sons of George Crosland

The sons and some of the other relatives lived in equally grand houses around Huddersfield, including Gledholt Hall, Thornton Lodge Hall, Birky Grange and Royds Hall.

Thomas Pearson Crosland (1815-1868), the eldest son, known as 'TP', lived at Gledholt Hall from 1852. He was Member of Parliament for Huddersfield in 1865 until his death in 1868. TP was a lieutenant-colonel in the Huddersfield Volunteers in 1864. As a young man he called himself a Liberal but later a Liberal-Conservative. T.P. Crosland had a son, also called T.P. Crosland (1856-1932). He lived at Birkby Grange and was a partner in the firm of George Crosland and Sons. He was a magistrate from 1886.

John Woodhead Crosland (1820-1882), George's second son, built Thornton Lodge Hall. This once grand house has been added to over the years and subdivided, so that it is quite difficult to see what it must have once looked like.

George's third son, Joseph (1826-1904), built himself a house across the Colne Valley from his family home; the house has been called Royds Wood and Royds Hall, in Paddock. The decoration that remains suggests it must have been a lovely house. In the 1881 Census, Joseph and his wife, Mary Ann Linton Fox, lived at the house with four servants. They had no children of their own. Maybe because of this, they took more of an interest in their nephews and nieces. Another of the family stories was that my great-grandmother, Kate Crosland, went on the Grand Tour with Sir Joseph and his wife. So far I have not been able to find any evidence to support this. Over the years Royds Hall has had several different uses, including a military hospital during the First World War. It became Huddersfield Grammar School in 1921, and is now Royds Hall School.

Joseph is perhaps the best known of the Croslands as he was knighted by Queen Victoria in 1889, as part of her seventieth birthday celebrations. Joseph had been educated privately, which probably meant at home with a tutor. He worked in the family firm, and participated in other commercial areas. He was elected Director of the Bank of Huddersfield in 1866 and Chairman from 1876 to 1897. He served as the first Conservative MP for Huddersfield from 1893 to 1895, and as a Justice of the Peace for Huddersfield and Deputy Lieutenant for the West Riding of Yorkshire in 1898. In 1898, Sir Joseph Crosland was made an Honorary Freeman of Huddersfield, in recognition of his services to civic life.

Joseph was also a benefactor of All Saints' church, Paddock, where he lived. He would have travelled frequently from his home to Crosland Moor Mills, passing All Saints', in Church Street, en route. He was churchwarden at All Saints' from 1875 to 1880 and again from 1884 to 1887. The church was originally built in the 1830s but was in need of restoration by the 1870s. Joseph layed the foundation stone for the Chancel and Vestries in 1878, having given over £3,600 for their construction. Mrs Joseph Crosland (*née* Mary Ann Linton Fox) gifted the painted glass for the East Window. When Sir Joseph died, friends gave a window in his memory.

In 1900, Joseph assisted The Bishop of Wakefield at the laying of the foundation stone at St Barnabas's church, in Crosland Moor. Earlier he had given a £1,000 donation to the Building Committee.

The Descendants of Thomas Crosland

Although the Croslands have left their mark on the town, those already mentioned are quite distant relatives to me, although the families seemed to have lived close to each other and their lives were interwoven. My family can trace its line back to Thomas and his wife Mary Ann Crosland, who was George Crosland's cousin. In 1851, according to the Census, he was the head of a family of woollen manufacturers, including James Crosland who was my great-great-grandfather.

James Crosland (1832-1913) built Royds Mount as a home for his family: a wife, one daughter and eight sons. James was the third son of Thomas and Mary Ann. James married the daughter of a Bradford woollen manufacturer, called Ann Bently, and it was as a result of this marriage that he was able

James Crosland and his family, 1890s.

Royd's Mount, home of James Crosland.

to build Royds Mount. James followed the family business as a woollen manufacturer, and had an office in Huddersfield off St Peter's Street. The woollen industry was not without its hazards, and a common hazard was fires. Trawling though the newspapers of the time, I found it surprising how many fires were reported. In 1888, a fire was reported at Millgate Mill, owned by James Crosland. Whether this contributed to the decline of the family's fortunes or not is hard to tell, but in 1899 James was declared bankrupt and the family home sold to the Crowthers.

Records of Civic Life

In Huddersfield Town Hall there are several huge wooden plaques which record the men who played a role in the civic life of Huddersfield at its creation as a borough in 1868. Painted in gold, alongside the names of the Mayor and his fellow councillors, is the name of Alderman James Crosland. He was the councillor for Marsh Ward.

James served on the Waterworks Corporation from its inception in 1868 and was rewarded for his long service by being asked to cut the first sod of the Butterley Reservoir in 1891. The silver and ebony spade that he used has been handed down the Crosland line to the present day. The Butterley Reservoir, four miles from Marsden, is one of a series of reservoirs which were built for the dual purpose of supplying domestic water to the rapidly growing population of Huddersfield in the mid-nineteenth century and also the water needed for the expanding wool processing and manufacturing industry. James was also a long-standing Justice of the Peace in Huddersfield.

Four of James's children married, including his daughter, Kate Crosland. Kate was my great-grandmother and she and her husband lived at The Holly, which until a few years ago stood on New Hey Road, Marsh. The Holly was demolished and some sheltered housing built on the site. Two unmarried sons emigrated to Canada (around 1913, after their father's death) and became champion sweet pea growers; one son died prematurely following an accident at Meltham Mills (1894) and another after a protracted illness.

Memorials

In St Peter's, Huddersfield's parish church, there is a memorial to T.P. Crosland and his family, but most of the family members have memorials in Edgerton Cemetery. There is a sameness about their memorials – all solid granite obelisks. The oldest one naturally records the life and death of George Crosland and his wife.

In 1874, James Crosland bought two adjacent grave spaces from the Corporation of Huddersfield for the sum of £10 10s, within the consecrated portion of the cemetery. This double plot provided sufficient space for sixteen members of the Crosland family to be interred together. The last Crosland to be interred was my grandmother's cousin, Sylvia, in 1992. She had lived in Huddersfield, ending her days in Reinwood Road, not so far from where her ancestors had first settled at Crosland Moor about 160 years previously.

Christine Piper

Richard Oastler: Champion of the Poor

'Man is free when he obeys the laws of morality which he finds within himself, and not in the external world'.

Immanuel Kant, *Groundwork to the Metaphysic of Morals*, 1785.

'My attention had not been particularly called to the subject of the factory children, until I had that fact communicated to me … I resolved from that moment that I would dedicate every power of mind and body to this object, until these poor children were relieved from that excessive labour, and from that moment, which was 29 September 1830, I have never ceased to use every legal means, which I had it in my power to use, for the purpose of emancipating these innocent slaves'.

Richard Oastler, giving evidence to a Parliamentary Select Committee about 'Yorkshire Slavery' in factories and mills, 1832.

The above quotations symbolise Richard Oastler's iron-willed determination to protect the poor and exploited workers of Britain's industrial towns during the first half of the nineteenth century. He was particularly distressed at the appalling treatment of child labourers within that draconian system. 'Thousands of little children from seven to fourteen years of age, are daily compelled to labour from six o'clock in the morning until eight o'clock at night, with only thirty minutes allowed for eating and recreation.'[1] Yet despite the moral strength of his argument, the man who became known as the 'Factory King' became the butt against which were aimed the poisoned arrows of his enemies – tyrannical mill-owners, 'Starvation Whigs' and their friends in the press. Each did their best to dampen Oastler's zeal, but without success. After all, here was a man who wrote to a fellow campaigner, 'Don't be alarmed at difficulties; all obstacles must and will give way.'[2]

Although he was born in Leeds on 29 September 1789, Oastler had such intimate relations with Huddersfield that the town can rightly call him her adopted son. Indeed, on

Boxing Day 1831, among the massed ranks of Huddersfield workers campaigning for a 'ten-hour day and a time-book' were witnessed a number of banners simply stating 'Oastler's Own'. Moreover, much of Oastler's effort to eradicate the cruelties that were endemic in an industrial system driven by the 'god of profit' stemmed from his personal witnessing of factory life in the Huddersfield area. 'I have seen little boys and girls,' he stated; 'One I have in my eye particularly now, whose forehead has been cut open by the thong; whose cheeks and lips have been laid open, and whose back has been almost covered with black stripes; and the only crime that that little boy had committed, was that he had retched three cardings...'[3]

But what drove this remarkable man to pursue the causes that he believed in so fervently at the risk of losing influential friends, personal security, and indeed liberty itself? After all, he was intelligent, charismatic, a Monarchist and a Tory. For nearly eighteen years between 1821 and 1838, he worked hard and diligently as Steward of Fixby Hall, Huddersfield, for the absentee landlord, Thomas Thornhill. He apparently perceived no irony when claiming, 'I believe loyalty to the Monarch and devotion to the poor are the first principles of divine truth.'[4] Indeed, Oastler's motto proclaimed the glory of 'The Altar, The Throne, and the Cottage.'[5] Yet still, he sacrificed domestic comfort with the 'whole-hearted co-operation and devoted solicitude of his beloved wife.'[6]

Certainly, Oastler must have been influenced in early life by his father's agitation on behalf of the ill-used and neglected chimney boys, on whom he spent much time and money.[7] Moreover, as early as 1807, he took up the anti-slavery question.[8] Also, however, Oastler was something of a Romanticist, preferring nature over culture, the organic over the mechanical, greater freedom for the individual, and all underpinned by the convictions of his faith. Like Immanuel Kant, he was critical of the pretensions of reason for the purpose of 'making room for faith'. It engendered within him a certain amount of irrationality. For instance, in a speech he made near Kirkgate, Huddersfield, he told a large crowd, 'I have seen ... a hand-loom which will enable you to compete with the power-looms and bring into your cottages domestic harmony and peace'.[9]

Undoubtedly, Oastler's Anglican religiosity encouraged him to repudiate the hypocritical Christianity of his enemies. Thus, in his opposition to the Poor Law Amendment Act of 1834, he raged: 'I cannot *bless* that, which GOD and NATURE curse. The Bible being true, the Poor Law Amendment Act is false!'[10] Clearly, these were the words of a man using the weapon of moral force in order to portray the Act as something alien to a purportedly religious elite.

Importantly, Oastler's religiosity did not deter him from forming alliances with anyone campaigning for the Ten-Hours' Day and against the Poor Law Amendment Act. Hence, the blossoming of his relationship with the Huddersfield Radicals. Explaining his reasons, he stated: 'I, being a Tory and a Churchman, and they Radicals and Dissenters, we agreed to work together, with the understanding that parties in politics and seats in religion should not be allowed to interfere between us.'[11] Thus, when a delegation from the Huddersfield Short-Time Committee went to Fixby Hall to invite Oastler to assume the leadership of their Movement, he accepted, despite reservations about their atheism. For the Committee, it was a great coup. As C. Driver observes, 'Oastler could do and say things that they could not; he had more leisure, more contacts, and more opportunities than they had'.[12] And so was born the famous 'Fixby Hall Compact' of June 1831.

F. Driver is wrong, however, to call the 'Compact' a myth, and that the Radicals' co-operation was 'less a matter of blind loyalty or ideological conviction than astute political calculation'.[13] It is true that many workers in Yorkshire and Lancashire were already in the struggle for factory reform when Oastler joined them, and that Radicals in Leeds disapproved of his candidature in Huddersfield for the General Elections of 1837, but the loyalty and affection of Huddersfield people towards him never wavered throughout his long battle for social justice.

No one should doubt that Oastler was not alone in agitating on behalf of the oppressed. Nevertheless, he was both the focal-point and the driving-force; fearless and unbending in his actions. Indeed, 'the great and good Bishop of Durham', Dr Van Mildert, asserted that Oastler was 'one who evidently feels that he has a mission to fulfil, and who … engages in that mission with all the ardour and self-sacrificing spirit of a martyr.'[14] In speech and letters, Oastler was never the most temperate, and thus made powerful enemies. But in response to critics of his aggressive style, he argued: 'I saw my young and helpless neighbours dying excruciatingly by inches under the lash and toil of the factory Monster; I heard their groans, I watched their tears, I knew they had relied on me'.[15] His mind had been set on helping factory children ever since his fateful meeting at the Bradford home of his good friend, John Wood (29 September, 1830). On the same day, he wrote a celebrated letter entitled 'Yorkshire Slavery' to the hostile *Leeds Mercury*,[16] 'thus starting a controversy which was to dominate most of the rest of his life'.[17]

At this juncture, Wood deserves to be recognized as one of the progenitors of Welfare Statism and the initiator of a ten-hour working day.[18] He was one of the wealthiest factory owners in England, yet a sensitive, somewhat retiring man, and, like Oastler, a Tory Churchman, 'given to charitable work'.[19] His employees were well cared for, with school rooms, a medical man, and good food in a factory canteen'.[20] It was he who actually drew Oastler's attention to the factory children's plight, and all the while provided the necessary finance to ensure the continuation of the campaign.[21]

Workers across the North were revitalized by Oastler's zeal, and at their revered 'King's' behest, they trudged fifty or sixty miles to York on the momentous Easter Pilgrimage in the cause of the Ten-Hours' Bill (24 April 1832). The Huddersfield group met in the Market Place and were joined by contingents from Honley, Holmfirth and other localities. There were bands and banners aplenty and, amidst a carnival atmosphere, the National Anthem was sung before the long hike started.[22] Along the route, they stopped in Leeds for refreshments and all the while were joined by other supporters. Finally, a crowd of 12,000 converged on York racecourse, exhausted and soaked as the weather deteriorated. On returning to Huddersfield, 'Oastler's Own' received a great reception. It is said that when Oastler reached Fixby Hall and removed his boots, 'the skin from his feet peeled off with his socks'.[23] He was not alone.

A month earlier, another of Oastler's friends, John Sadler MP, had introduced into the House of Commons a Ten-Hours' Bill, but as a delaying tactic, Parliament appointed a Select Committee to investigate factory conditions. Oastler was not fooled. Of such Commissions he raged, 'They are coming to seek Billy-Rollers and Straps when they are all put sideways! They are coming to seek for the victims of avarice above ground whom Death has mercifully hidden under ground! ... They won't catch Mill-lasses with young Masters, and old ones too (say HOGGS if you like!) in the Counting house and Warehouse when they come!'[24]

The Select Committee convened in London. Prominent people such as the Revd George C. Bull from Bradford, Michael Sadler MP and Oastler himself spoke with fearless eloquence in defence of the downtrodden factory workers – especially for the child labourers. But the victims brought their own poignant witness. This, for instance, is part of Joseph Habergam's testimony : 'I reside at Northgate, Huddersfield. I began to work when seven years old at George Addison's, Bradley Mills, Huddersfield.... I had fourteen and a half hours' actual labour a day ... and I received as wages two-and-six a week'.[25] Another witness, Mark Best, stated that children were 'fined for combing their hair before they went home, or washing themselves'.[26]

Evidence supporting the need for a shorter working day and the protection of child labourers seemed overwhelming. However, the General Election of 1832 cut short the Select Committee's proceedings, Sadler lost his seat in Government, and thereafter, the elites continued to thwart reform, believing that it would erode the profits of mill-owners and damage Britain's economic competitiveness.

A weary Oastler took the Hope Coach from London to Huddersfield, and was met by a large crowd in Kirkgate. He immediately retired to his favourite inn, the Rose and Crown, where a band of musicians greeted him. On emerging from the inn suitably refreshed, he gave a rousing speech, which included a typically defiant stab at the tyrannical mill-owners: 'Instead of punishing the Master that breaks the law with a fine only, punish him with a fine and imprisonment, set him in the pillory, put him in the stocks, and if you do that I will bound your Bill will be effected enough' (crowd laughter and applause).[27]

As long as he lived, Oastler never gave up the fight for the emancipation of the factory children and the poor. It eventually led to his dismissal as Steward of Fixby Hall following his resistance to the implementation of the new Poor Law Act in Huddersfield (1838). Worse was to come. During his time working for Mr Thornhill, 'he treated the tenantry and the poor in a generous and almost royal way'.[28] It led to him owing his boss about £2,000. Nevertheless, Thornhill agreed to take a promissory note for the debt, which it was understood, Oastler was to reduce annually. Unfortunately, his enemies persuaded Thornhill to call in the debt, and consequently, Oastler – being unable to pay – was incarcerated in Fleet Prison from 9 December 1840 until his release on 12 February 1844. As Chadwick notes, 'he was imprisoned ostensibly for debt but actually in order to suppress the movement for factory reform'.[29] Oastler had been in prison hardly a month before his 'Huddersfield Boys' held an 'Oastler Festival' in the Philosophical Hall. There was a high tea followed by a concert and dance attended by over 600 people. A cheque for over £23 went to the Fleet as a result.[30]

From prison, Oastler wrote to Thornhill, 'The Poor Law Commissioners have succeeded in dishonouring you. They have told you that I was your enemy; when they said so, they well knew that they deceived you'.[31]

Preceding his release, he wrote to his great friend, Lawrence Pitkethly, 'I need retire for rest, to the North Riding; they want a public dinner there – but I say no – Huddersfield

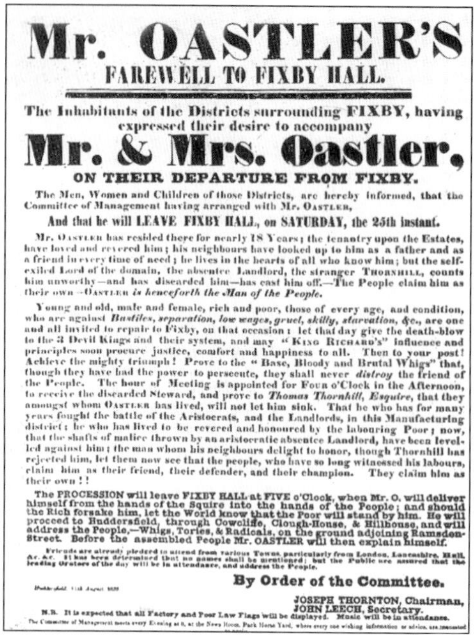

Mr. OASTLER'S
FAREWELL TO FIXBY HALL.

The Inhabitants of the Districts surrounding FIXBY, having expressed their desire to accompany

Mr. & Mrs. Oastler,
ON THEIR DEPARTURE FROM FIXBY.

The Men, Women and Children of those Districts, are hereby informed, that the Committee of Management having arranged with Mr. Oastler,

And that he will LEAVE FIXBY HALL, on SATURDAY, the 25th instant.

Mr. Oastler has resided there for nearly 18 Years; the tenantry upon the Estates, have loved and revered him; his neighbours have looked up to him as a father and as a friend in every time of need; he lives in the hearts of all who know him; but the self-exiled Lord of the domain, the absentee Landlord, the stranger Thornhill, counts him unworthy—and has discarded him—has cast him off.—The People claim him as their own—Oastler *is henceforth the Man of the People.*

Young and old, male and female, rich and poor, those of every age, and condition, who are against *Bastiles, separation, low wages, gruel, skilly, starvation, &c.*, are one and all invited to repair to Fixby, on that occasion: let that day give the death-blow to the 3 Devil Kings and their system, and may "King Richard's" influence and principles soon procure justice, comfort and happiness to all. Then to your post! Achieve the mighty triumph! Prove to the "Base, Bloody and Brutal Whigs" that, though they have had the power to persecute, they shall never *distroy* the friend of the People. The hour of Meeting is appointed for Four o'Clock in the Afternoon, to receive the discarded Steward, and prove to *Thomas Thornhill, Esquire*, that they amongst whom Oastler has lived, will not let him sink. That he who has for many years fought the battle of the Aristocrats, and the Landlords, in this Manufacturing district; he who has lived to be revered and honoured by the labouring Poor; now, that the shafts of malice thrown by an aristocratic absentee Landlord, have been levelled against him; the man whom his neighbours delight to honor, though Thornhill has rejected him, let them now see that the people, who have so long witnessed his labours, claim him as their friend, their defender, and their champion. They claim him as their own!!

The PROCESSION will leave FIXBY HALL at FIVE o'Clock, when Mr. O. will deliver himself from the hands of the Squire into the hands of the People; and should the Rich forsake him, let the World know that the Poor will stand by him. He will proceed to Huddersfield, through Cowcliffe, Clough-House, & Hillhouse, and will address the People,—Whigs, Tories, & Radicals, on the ground adjoining Ramsden-Street. Before the assembled People Mr. OASTLER will then explain himself.

Friends are already pledged to attend from various Towns, particularly from London, Lancashire, Hull, &c. &c. It has been determined that no names shall be mentioned; but the Public are assured that the leading Orators of the day will be in attendance, and address the People.

By Order of the Committee.

JOSEPH THORNTON, Chairman,
JOHN LEECH, Secretary.

N.B. It is expected that all Factory and Poor Law Flags will be displayed. Music will be in attendance.

The Committee of Management meets every Evening at 8, at the News Room, Pack Horse Yard, where every one wishing information or advice, are requested

first'.[32] And so it was. He arrived at Brighouse by train from Leeds on Shrove Tuesday, 20 February 1844. The procession to Huddersfield was 'without precedent in local history. The ovation which he received from the people demonstrated that his long absence had not diminished their affection.'[33] On arrival at Queen Street, a band played 'See the Conquering Hero Comes'. Following a speech by Oastler, the proceedings were brought to a close with, 'three cheers for the Queen and three unutterable curses for the Metropolitan police'.[34]

The culmination of the Ten-Hours' Movement came with the Ten-Hours' Act of 1847, but poor drafting meant that employers could easily side-step the new laws. The clear ten hours were only secured in 1874.[35]

Richard Oastler, the 'Factory King', died of a heart attack on a visit to Harrogate on 22 August 1861. At his funeral, the coffin containing his remains was carried by specially selected factory workers from Yorkshire and Lancashire, and was laid to rest in the crypt of Kirkstall church, Leeds. In life, he did have certain faults. His opposition to Catholic emancipation and universal suffrage in Britain is hard to reconcile with his great efforts on behalf of the brutalized factory children and the poor. And his belief that industrialization could somehow revert to family cottage industries was somewhat naïve. Nevertheless, his fearless struggle to improve the condition of the working classes, and his passionate fight against child slavery in England's dark Satanic mills, marks him as a truly extraordinary man.

At Christ Church, Woodhouse, the church where the Oastler family had regularly worshipped during their residence at Fixby Hall, there is a monument to Oastler's memory, lovingly paid for by Huddersfield workers. The playground at Greenhead Park is also dedicated to him, while in Bradford, there is a statue of him with two of his adoring factory children. But really, the town of Huddersfield should do more to commemorate a man who sacrificed so much in the name of humanity. The magnificent bronze statue of Harold Wilson[36] outside the Huddersfield railway station should be matched by a similar tribute to Oastler in a suitable central location.

For end notes please see pp. 35-36.

Peter Breban

Ada's Christmas Eve, 1926

Christmas Eve 1926 is etched forever in the memory of Ada Marston. Then Miss Truelove, she had a friend, Violet, whose acquaintance she had made at chapel. Violet was of outsize proportions. So much so that she had to wear men's boots when working in service at the rectory. Her feet really required seven league boots.

Her clothes were protected with an ancient harding apron, tied round her ample form with black tapes. Ada thought her friend looked like the back end of a bus, but being a chapel goer and brought up to be charitable, she put that thought aside and accepted an invitation to tea with Violet and her parents. In a basement dwelling by the River Colne, Violet was engaged for twenty-three years, but like so many at that time, felt they must look after their parents. Edith, Ada's sister, was also invited, as was Josiah Jackson, a local preacher. Mrs White, Violet's mother, had baked some date pasty. She put it outside by the drain to cool off. 'Nay, mother, you couldn't have put it in a more unhygienic place' complained Violet. 'Right big, was Mrs White,' recalled Ada, 'Twenty stones at least, with three double chins,' Her husband was always known as 'Old White' and was a bit lewd; he was 'a ganger by trade.'

Seated round the tea table down that mucky sort of lane leading to some mills and near the canal, Old White (Edith told her sister later) had grabbed hold of her knee, underneath the table cloth. 'Well, you couldn't be in accordance with that sort of carry-on' related Ada, so Edith made some excuse, probably a headache and went off home. Mrs White hacked a piece of pasty for the parson, there were no niceties in that house, and Josiah Jackson began to choke, a date stone having logged in his throat.

Ada, the only one with any presence of mind, thumped him on his back and when nothing happened tried to comfort the distraught man of God by assuring him that 'in the course of time and nature,' he would part with it. 'Put your hand down your throat' Ada suggested, but it was useless; he was unable to preach that evening. It was agreed that Ada, an occasional lay preacher, give a little talk before the late night carol singing.

Then Old Man White made a decision. 'Your father would be sickened if he thought you were having to walk home at dead of night,' he told Ada as he adjusted the flickering gas bracket. 'You'd better stay here with us. Violet sleeps on the horsehair sofa, you can pig in with us.'

Ada had never pigged in with anyone before, let alone strangers and a married couple of gigantic proportions. But she dutifully went off into the night with the rest of the chapel carol singers, pausing every now and again for a glass of ginger wine and a slice of spice cake at various hovels and cottages along the way. Half of the householders were blotto, it being

Ada Truelove in the 1920s.

Christmas Eve, and none of the singers were exactly Caruso or Clara Butt. More like crackpots grovelling up and down, recalled the nineteen-year-old Ada. 'It was foreign to me, all that kind of carrying on.'

Worse was to come, at bedtime when the carol singing was over. Ada was handed one of her hostess's nightgowns, so commodious that it wrapped round her slight form umpteen times. Everything was in the one basement room. Yorkshire range, sink, horsehair sofa, the shut-up bed against the wall. With a glint in his eye Old White yanked it down. He didn't use his handkerchief much and looked, according to Ada, 'sackless.' Both he and his wife had great big swollen legs and sweaty feet. But Violet was oblivious of all that was going on as soon as the blankets were up to her nose.

Both her parents had creaky joints that needed attention, and the bedclothes stank of oil of wintergreen. It had saturated the blankets many moons ago. But they seemed happy as pigs in muck. Mrs White heaved herself onto the bed. 'You lie at the side of me.' She indicated a few inches for Ada, who hesitated, but it was a case of Hobson's choice. It was pitch dark outside, and once the gas was put out, the same inside. She lay stiff and rigid with cold, having given up any hope of keeping any covering, foul as it was, on her side of the bed, When dawn came at long last her eyes felt like bullets from lack of sleep, and hearing frequent rattling in the chamber pot beneath the bed.

'Did you have to go?' I asked. 'Well, we know people have to go, give due respects, but I wouldn't have known which direction to take in that pitch blackness. Besides, thankfully, I was younger then, so the occasion didn't arise.' But on reflection, 'it put paid to my Christmas dinner,' she smiled. After thanking her hosts for providing shelter that Christmas Eve, Ada thankfully made her getaway, walking home to her widowed father and sister Edith. Mr Truelove pronounced the episode 'a bit of a dagger' in the terminology of the twenties.

A few years later Edith married, and Violet acquired a big fur with proper tail and head with glaring eyes from a jumble sale. 'Is it a fox fur?' Ada asked with awe. 'Oh no, it's a goat skin and glass eyes put in to complete the picture.' The clasp mustn't have been right good as it slid off

Herbert Truelove and Gypsy the dog in the 1920s.

Ada in the 1930s.

so there was nothing for it but to wear a pair of her late father's old white cricket boots beneath the white wedding gown. Nobody knew but Ada.

If this Christmas is problematical, don't despair, it could be worse. Just remember 1926 in the West Riding of Yorkshire, and being in a shut-up bed with Old White and his twenty-stone wife, and no heavenly scents of pot pourri and pine cones, but an overpowering stench of stale wintergreen. Then you'll know for certain, that Christmas could be worse.

Hazel Wheeler

A Quiet Man and a Poet

The *Huddersfield Daily Examiner* has two photographs of Fred Brown in its archives. One, from 1976, shows him with pen poised over a notepad. He looks frail, dignified, with a slight smile. He wears a comfortable cardigan and open-necked shirt; he could be the man next door who likes growing potatoes. The piece brings out his very human, ordinary side. It comments that he likes autograph-hunting and that the pride of his signatures is that of Bing Crosby.

However, he is featured in the local paper because he has been made an honorary member of the Yorkshire Dialect Society. He is ranked with the Archbishop of Canterbury and J.B. Priestley in his position of vice-president of the society. Even more impressive is the 1977 feature. This marks the moment when Fred was made an honorary fellow of the International Poetry Society. This time he

when Violet heaved into the church and swept up the aisle. The next person following ended up wiping his feet on it, his eyes being focused on the altar.

Violet had been entrusted with the task of making sandwiches for the wedding party beforehand. 'And more dropped on t'floor than t'table,' moaned the bride's father. However, 'The Good Book', as always, was open on a small table alongside, and 'well, it could have been worse,' all agreed.

When eventually Old White and his wife passed on to better things than shut-up beds and oil of wintergreen, Violet was free at last to become a wife. Her feet were still of outsize proportions, and no wedding shoes could be found anywhere,

Fred Brown in a photograph from the Daily Examiner, *16 March 1977, after his election as a Fellow of the International Poetry Society. The caption reads, 'Writer, broadcaster and poet, Mr Brown is a retired power-loom overlooker. He is a vice-president of the Yorkshire Dialect Society. He is eighty-three and, as our picture shows, enjoys carving. Among the few fellows of the IPS are William Alwyn, Kingsley Amis and the Czechoslovak poet, Ondra Lysohorsky.*

shares his fame with such writers as Kingsley Amis.

Yet this celebrated poet, who broadcast on local radio and lived for almost eighty years in Huddersfield (most of these years in Moor End Road, Lockwood), died a lonely figure, with only two people at his funeral. One of those mourners was Arthur Kinder, and his story of the funeral, as told by local writer Ken Edward Smith, has led me to attempt a reappraisal of Fred Brown's life.

The story of the funeral is that Arthur met the vicar before the service, and he knew nothing of Fred Brown's personality. Arthur Kinder informed him, and they both walked into an empty crematorium chapel. In a strange way, such a sad and quiet exit from life seems in keeping with the nature of a very quiet, private and self-contained man.

Fred Brown (1893-1980) was a remarkable man in many respects, but it was his late fame as a dialect poet that has made him a Huddersfield celebrity. He published only three slim collections: *Songs of the Factory and Loom* (1943), *More Songs of the Factory and Loom* (1947) and *The Muse Went Weaving* (1972). His work attracted the notice of a publisher in Bakewell, Hub Publications, in the 1970s, and the Yorkshire Dialect Society also promoted his work, seeing that his skill in dialect writing was a rare combination of poetic expertise and the authentic feel of a locality. Everything he wrote was rooted in the reality of daily work and leisure. His life was mostly spent in and around Huddersfield, although he was born in Keighley. Ken Edward Smith has written about Fred's life and notes that Fred was born into a family 'deeply involved in the local worsted textile industry.'[1]

His father was a power loom tuner and Fred eventually followed the same trade, after taking courses at Huddersfield Technical College, his family having moved to Huddersfield when Fred was only seven. He was apprentice with Taylor and Livesey at Lockwood, and at this time he married Bessie Ardson. The few people in the Huddersfield area now who still recall Fred refer to his later work at Eccles and Watson on Firth Street, and the person they remember was a quiet man. Ken Edward Smith has commented that Fred was a 'somewhat lonely figure alternating between hospital and old peoples' homes.'[2] Research has highlighted other aspects of this remarkable man's life; in fact, there is a great deal to be drawn from the bare outline of his life, and the deduction involved adds more conviction that his poetry is of lasting value.

The Fred Brown recalled by workmates is a warm, approachable person. In his role of power loom tuner, he is remembered by Kathleen Milnes, a worker at Firth Street who retired in 1975. Kathleen, the daughter of a coachman at Longley Hall, says that he was a quiet man, very reliable, who 'didn't talk unnecessarily, like some do'. He was a thoughtful superior at work, she remarks, as he looked after the women workers. She stresses that 'in 1941 for instance, at the height of the war, we were working twelve hours a day and there wasn't much money about. Fred made sure we had good pay – not brilliant, but he never wasted any time.' Their wages depended on him. Such memories are testimonies of love and affection. Fred was obviously a responsible, disciplined and reliable worker, despite the fact that he thought mill-work a demanding, tiring job; his poems set in the weaving industry do stress the tough, physically stressful nature of the work.

He was a 'quiet man' with whom Kathleen would often walk to work down Firth Street after Fred left his bus and their walks were often silent but companionable. He showed his poetry books at work. It was the physical environment of the workplace that gave his writing its power and authentic feel. His poem 'Sins and Shins' typifies this. It refers to the process of healding, in which a 'reacher-in', who was a young boy, passed a warp-end through the healds. In former times, a sleepy reacher-in was given a kick. This is Fred's poem:

'At Sunday school
They allus said
Forgive men all their sins.
Ah carn't forgive
Old healder Ben,
For poising me mi shins.[3]

This is so embedded in working life that the son of George Cartwright, the man who used to kick Fred's shins, knows the autobiographical basis of the poem. Peter Cartwright gave me a remarkable image of Fred in his workplace and of the tuner's responsibility. Fred told George (who retired in 1955) that the 'Ben' of the poem was really him. Peter recalls Fred only from a child's perspective, but defines the tuner's work in this way: 'He looked after the looms – a sort of mechanic – and if you went into a mill and saw the tuner sat down, you knew you were in a good mill.' In my conversation with Peter Cartwright, he guessed that Fred probably wrote some of the first drafts of his poems at those times when he could sit down in between duties.

There is another side to Fred Brown's life, however, and tracing this is a difficult task. His son, Alec, emigrated to Canada in 1954, and Fred's only friends appear to have been people who knew him at the local writers' group or from his work in dialect writing. But Fred had done other things, and played his part in modern history. In the First World War he had joined the Royal Cycle Corps as a volunteer; the primary duties were carrying messages. Yet he must have seen a great deal of action. The cycles were attached to supporting services, and were usually a part of the cavalry division, there being thirty-three bicycles in support for communications duties. It seems entirely typical of Fred's life that there is very little in the war literature about the activities of the Cycle Corps. It seems that, as a soldier in an ancillary capacity, he viewed the events with a broad, reflective perspective. He saw service in Greece, and in his later poetry, war becomes a central theme. Certainly, such a wartime role would have been grist to the mill for a writer of such detachment and contemplation as Fred was to become. Whatever experiences he had, and there is nothing explicit in print on this, it certainly had a profound effect on his view of mankind; a rage against man's inhumanity to man is at the heart of many poems in his main collection. His work often deals with the nature of hatred and war, even to the point of linking the actual physical nature of blood to thoughts of Cain and Abel (in the poem 'Blood Transfusion'). Fred's father married Anna Render (the daughter of an industrialist) and they had five children. Fred was the eldest son. His brother Harry was successful as a businessman and established the Rustless Curtain Rod Company of Batley. Fred was employed as secretary until he moved to his intended career in the mills. The family move to Honley, and then to Lockwood, and these places clearly exposed Fred Brown to some varieties of Yorkshire speech which were to implant that deep source of creativity so evident in his unfaltering perception of real dialogue. In his poems, he loves to explore the articulations of working-class speech and this provides a rare stylistic strength to his treatment of quite familiar subjects.

He also experienced the Depression, of course, and he was out of work for eighteen months. At one point, when he was involved in a strike centred on the powerloom tuners, things were so tough that Fred's wife actually cooked food to sell to the workers in the area. During the '40s he became an observer for the Mass Observation organization led by Charles Madge and Tom Harrisson, who wanted 'untrained observers as these would be subjective cameras each with his or her own distortion.'[4] The Mass Observation appeal for observers was made in a Penguin Special paperback in 1939, and Fred must have responded to that. In Valentine Cunningham's definitive work on British Writers of the Thirties, we have an explanation of the historical context and of Fred's part in the movement: 'Notably, M-O also provided an outlet for striving and ambitious would-be writers.... It's not at all surprising to discover that the Huddersfield power-loom tuner was Fred Brown, author of *The Muse Went Weaving*.'[5]

As Cunningham comments, it was literary types who signed up. Clearly, in that period of the little magazines, and of renewed interest in regional writing, exemplified by the *Northern Review* from Leeds, Fred Brown was keen to be published. Perhaps his Standard English writing never made the impact that his dialect writing did. In the *Northern Review* for 1947, for instance, many of the contributors made reputations as 'Yorkshire writers': there are such names as Gordon Allen North and Allan Prior in that edition.[6] This was at the same time as Fred Brown was self-publishing his booklet of poetry; the dialect writing which brought him success was still to come into prominence.

The Mass Observation work suited his talents and interests admirably. It simply involved logging the minutiae of everyday life in the mill and indeed in the town generally. The lists of subjects for note given by the Mass Observation editors range from the relatively banal (behaviour of people at war memorials) to the deeply significant (attitudes to anti-semitism). Fred Brown's brief was mainly industrial. In fact, the habit of surveying attitudes and social life in West Yorkshire remained popular with publishers up to the mid-1960s, when, ironically, a book detailing a variety of Yorkshire working people included a profile of a Mr Kinder, who was perhaps related to Fred's friend, Arthur Kinder. Recent anthologies of Mass Observation writing, such as Angus Calder and Dorothy Sheridan's *Speak for Yourself* (published by Cape in 1984) show the template for the local observations (although they use Blackpool as the model). Fred would have been walking Huddersfield with notepad in hand, and his ear for conversation would have made him an ideal social witness to the 'new Britain'.

There is some uncertainty about when he actually started writing poetry. Evidence is scarce, and study of his work immediately post-1945 has involved some inference and speculation. All the verbal evidence, in his poems and in oral testimony from people who knew him, suggests that he was deeply at odds with modernity, and was often critical of change for its own sake. His insistent, elegiac voice in his lyrics indicates a man who reflected deeply and resented anything threatening mankind. He was encouraged early on by Robin Gregory, of Hub Publications in Bakewell, Derbyshire. This was a turning-point in Fred's progress towards a certain local fame and to his honours in the wider poetry community. At that time, the late 1970s, it was unusual for a dialect writer to attract interest in the literary magazines, most of which specialized in Standard English writing only, and considered dialect writing to be largely the province of either amateur doggerel-scribblers or of lovable eccentrics who were happy with a very small, regional readership. Fred's work was highly successful in making

that crossing from dialect to mainstream in modern poetry. His work began to appear in a range of small magazines, and his name was noticed by practitioners of all varieties of writing. The reviews were generally favourable.

Fred Brown wrote about Huddersfield people and local settings, and he chose to include a tough sinew of dialect in the syntax. His collection needs a glossary, and the poems would be hard work for readers outside Yorkshire, but only for a short while, and concentration would bring a fine reward. His success may be explained with reference to the tradition of West Riding dialect poetry and the distinction often made between 'poetry' and 'versifying'. The latter may be close to doggerel and rely only

The cover for Fred's collection, The Muse Went Weaving *(Hub/Yorkshire Dialect Society).*

on insistent and often clumsy rhymes. In the foreword to *The Muse Went Weaving*, Wilfrid J. Halliday makes this point: 'There are many versifiers in dialect – some of them excellent within their own scope – but Fred has a consistently poetic view of life, and his readers share his vision.'[7]

There are arguably two parallel traditions of dialect writing: one stems from the popular Victorian and Edwardian almanacs and the other is more engaged in mingling realistic speech intonation and conversation into lyric poetry. The former is often sentimental and narrative; the latter uses dialect as an emotional centre formed from expressive style. Fred Brown is in the second tradition. In his short lyrics such as 'T'Shadder Show', about a fire in Atkinson's cotton mills at Colne Bridge in 1818, he shows how he could use conventional poetic vocabulary by the side of colloquial Yorkshire (a scray is a wooden platform):

'A *young lad whistled as he loaded a scray:*
A ghost-child smiled as it donced away.'[8]

Considering how much dialect writing has remained firmly in the ranks of ephemera, and how much has been written (necessarily) for a minority local readership, Fred Brown's poetry has remained available and indeed celebrated. In the recent celebratory paperback from the Yorkshire Dialect Society, *A Century of Yorkshire Dialect*, Fred Brown is represented by several poems. His poetry has helped to establish a connection with the dialect verse of past Huddersfield writing – a body of work that was often part of working-class identity and aspiration. This convention was always linked to the recital and public reading, of course, and it is clear that Fred Brown enjoyed reading his poems. In an age in which so much literary work has no link to performance and community sense, we have

to look to the dialect writers to remind us of a kind of regional history in which such writing was significant for almost everyone. The subjects of his poems usually relate to ideas of change and the community. Often, he takes a simple object as a way into understanding continuity and historical process, as in 'Breaking Point' in which the breaking of an ancient cup leads to anti-war statements done with a rare power and simplicity:

'An *then ah thowt*
O' t'lumps o' clay,
Wi' t'breath o' life
God quickened;
Then half-wit men
Goa smash 'em up…'

Fred Brown's work will continue to be valued as an important landmark in the continuity of dialect writing. As long ago as 1914, writers were expressing some doubts as to whether dialect writing in the local publications was actually representing the ordinary Yorkshire folk. In fact, Fred's writing has been singled out for special praise by critics and reviewers because he manages to do what many have tried but few have achieved in dialect writing: to handle both descriptive social comment and more profound and universal themes. Many of the short meditation poems aspire to the depth of insight normally found in Elizabethan lyric verse. His poems do this by the plain but subtle use of the natural landscape, and we have the feel of the moors and trees in his local topography in the best of these, such as these lines from 'Frost Pictures':

'A *fey frosty hand,*
Wi' nowt much to gain,
Plants aeons o' growth
On a rimed window pane.'

In Fred Brown's poetry, there is no doubt that he achieved that convincing sense of close knowledge of his subjects. The quiet man in the mill was a good friend, and also an ideal fieldworker for Mass Observation. In that paradox we have a case of a man who had two distinct lives in one: the listener and the active, involved writer about his own piece of Yorkshire. Trying to trace the contours of his life is like a journey through a foggy network of dark streets. He was an example of that type of writer who is 'deep' and quiet as a workmate, but who observes closely and transmutes this attentiveness into a special art. He may prove to be one of Yorkshire's outstanding poets, and we will lament the fact that he did not write more than the poems in the few slim volumes. In fact, as I hope I have shown, there was perhaps another writer in him: one who could have said much more about history in the national sense, but instead, he kept quiet about such things and remained a poet of Huddersfield.

For end notes please see p. 36.

Stephen Wade

Dorothy Wood

Introduction

Never have so many in Marsden, the Colne Valley and Huddersfield owed so much to one woman.

Miss Dorothy Wood was a Huddersfield nurse who gave so much to the health and welfare of mothers and new born infants, only for her own life to end in tragedy. She spent her professional career helping other women and children. Her career spanned twenty-seven years as a nurse, delivering infant, child health and welfare services as a school nurse and health visitor in the Colne

Valley. She was not unique, as another nurse, Mrs S.E. Haynes, the school nurse and Queen's District Nurse for Canterbury for twenty years, was instrumental in starting the Canterbury School Clinic[1]. Long service records in health care were not uncommon in this period of labour history. Often health visitor/school nurse roles were combined for effective deployment of staff and they often worked in the same area for considerable numbers of years.[2] However, Miss Wood's contribution to maternal and child health in Huddersfield continued the earlier pioneering work in public health.[3,4,5] These accounts of the development of public health, and particularly infant welfare, services in Huddersfield during the early twentieth century show the important role played by Huddersfield in national child welfare policy development. The growth of eighteenth and nineteenth-century local health care has been previously documented.[6,7] The first half of the twentieth century is considered by reviewing Miss Wood's career. Her murder provides a sad conclusion to her life.

Miss Dorothy Wood

Dorothy Wood was born on 13 August 1901.[8] She was a very good school pupil, according to her 1917 school report[9], certificate and exam result.[10] After leaving school it is unclear what she did, but in the early 1920s she trained as a nurse at St Luke's Poor Law Infirmary in Halifax.[11] Around 1924-1925 she completed her training and worked for the Halifax King Edward VII Memorial Nursing Association based in Clare Road, Halifax, where she gained her Central Midwives Board and Queen's District Nursing Certificates. Here she spent four years working as a Queen's Nurse.[12] Later she went on six months' study

Miss Dorothy Wood. (Huddersfield Daily Examiner)

staff consisted of 1 Superintendent, 1 Assistant Superintendent, 7 General Nurses, 4 Midwives and 4 Pupils.[18]

Marsden

Marsden probably means boundary valley or 'at the head of the Colne Valley' and 'surrounded by hills.' It was a thriving textile town at its industrial peak but 'Marsden is no longer a textile township as there are only three mills now in operation.'[19]

Marsden District Nursing Association was formed in 1920 and its members, on payment of a small annual subscription, had the service of a resident nurse, Nurse Prentice,[20] who by 1932 was making 2,537 annual visits.[21] Before Miss Wood moved to Marsden, the West Riding County Council opened the maternity and child welfare centre on 1st December 1927 at Marsden Conservative Club. This provided free advice to mothers about their health and that of their children. A doctor and nurse attended each Thursday afternoon and some ladies formed a committee volunteering to sell baby food, weigh babies, keep records, and provide tea for the mothers and staff. Twelve months before, Mrs Laura Hampshire and Mrs Jessie Bamforth had sold child welfare foods, provided by the County Council, at the Mechanics' Hall. Mrs Hampshire became Secretary of the Committee, and brought baby foods from the manufacturers for sale at the clinic and on average eighty mothers and babies were seen weekly.[22] The first village nurse was Nurse Currie who later resigned on 6 March 1929.[23] The clinic nurses arranged annual outings to Blackpool and local beauty spots.[24]

Arrival at Marsden

Following her course at Leeds University it

for the new Health Certificate at Leeds University,[13,14] which is confirmed by the Ladies' Committee minutes of 2 October 1928: 'A new Nurse has been engaged in place of Miss Wood, who is taking a course at Leeds University.'[15] Furthermore, 'Several of our Nurses besides being fully trained have passed the Examination set by the Queen's Institute and are therefore entitled to be called "Queen's Nurses". One of them is now taking a course at the Leeds University and hopes to take up health visiting later on.'[16]

In 1929, the Halifax District Nursing Association's staff made 17,902 visits.[17] The is not clear why Dorothy Wood chose to move to Marsden in 1929. However, on 5 June 1929 the County Medical Officer reported that 'he had, with the approval of the chairman, temporarily appointed Miss Dorothy Wood, of Huddersfield, to act as Child Welfare Nurse in Marsden starting at £160 per year' and the meeting confirmed her appointment.[25] Coincidentally, 1929 was recognized as the beginning of a new era of health care both at local and national levels.[26]

On arrival at Marsden, Miss Wood worked in two Slaithwaite and three Marsden schools. She ran clinics and school inspections, keeping a watchful eye on children from the tender age of fourteen days until the end of their school life.[27] In 1930 the schools were reorganized: the National School became the Junior School and the Council School became the Marsden Senior School.[28] At retirement, a tribute to Miss Wood recalled: 'At this time the Child Welfare Centre and Clinic had only just been established and very few mothers attended. But under her leadership members flocked to the clinic and it is largely due to her hard work that it has become the thriving centre it is today.'[29]

Canada Scholarship

In 1932 Miss Wood entered a College of Nursing scholarship award from the Halifax sub-branch. The closing date for entries was 30 April, and, after sitting the competitive exam on Saturday 21 May, and being interviewed, Miss Wood was awarded the scholarship and went on a six-month trip to Canada to study Health Visiting at Montreal and Toronto.[30,31]

It was reported that 'The County Council values her services so highly they are keeping open her post until she returns'.[32]

The County Medical Officer reported that 'Nurse D. Wood had obtained a scholarship of £50 for a post-graduate course,' and that 'six months' leave of absence without salary [would] be granted'.[33] This was extended to 1 May 1933.[34] The scholarship covered her travelling expenses and she was provided with excellent hospitality while there.[35]

The West Riding County Council was praised for its 'sympathy and encouragement' in dealing with Miss Wood.[36] The Committee was not always generous; an earlier request from Nurse Airey, Health Visitor and School Nurse, for a grant to attend an educational visit to Germany organized by the Women Sanitary Inspectors' and Health Visitors' Association was refused. She was allowed to attend at her own expense with leave out of her annual holidays. At the same meeting, however, a County Alderman and the County Medical Officer were allowed to attend a National Conference on Maternity and Child Welfare in London in July 1930 and to have their expenses paid.[37]

Miss Wood's reputation is best summed up by this account of her: 'All who have watched her career have been impressed by her enthusiasm for her work. She has had remarkable success in all her examinations, and, better still, excellent reports from those in authority.'[38] She left for Canada on 21 October 1932.[39] It is reported that she 'sailed to Canada full of anticipation of the many new things she would learn,' and was 'naturally delighted at the prospect of such a long trip, and said she hoped she would have a receptive mind to assimilate all the things she saw'.[40] A number of archival documents suggest she represented Huddersfield, nursing and the country very well. She was very well received and made many friends.[41] In a Canadian newspaper she expresses a 'particular interest in the toxoiding of children as a diphtheria preventative' and states she 'would endeavour to induce the Yorkshire authorities to start a similar campaign.' There is no evidence that this happened.[42]

Two *Nursing Times* articles during 1933 provide accounts of her Canadian experiences. She is quoted as 'enjoying a wonderful programme of public health experience.' She noted 'the great difference is that there are no nurses' homes, each nurse having her own apartment and using the district headquarters merely as an office'. She further comments that in the office 'a vast amount of clerical work is done. I was appalled by the number of records kept.'[43] She describes a 'quite a thrilling experience' when, 'the doctor called for us with his car to attend a maternity case about fifteen miles away. We arrived at the case in good time, and I bathed the newest little Canadian.' She concludes, 'Thus will come to a close my tour of inspection and education. I shall frequently recall with great pleasure the hospitality received, the privileges extended and the experiences enjoyed during these memorable six months in Canada.'[44] An undated Christmas card from Gorden P. Jackson, Minister of Health, Toronto, illustrates the impact of her visit.[45] She presented a written report to the College of Nursing in London on 4 November 1933.[46] That year Miss M. Chapman won the scholarship, using it to learn massage.[47]

After returning from Canada she settled back into working in Marsden and the Colne Valley. In the early 1930s she was receiving an annual pay rise of £10, from £190 in 1933-1934 to £210 in 1935-1936.[48]

In December 1935 a serious outbreak of diphtheria with three fatalities occurred, which shows the sort of diseases she was dealing with,[49] despite public health lectures with titles such as 'keeping babies alive' being offered at the temperance Hall on Thursday nights,[50] and free immunization which had been available since 1931.[51] In 1933 Marsden made determined efforts to stop the disease spreading from local areas, its clinic inoculating 244 children from three schools on Wednesday 29 December 1933.[52] By 1938 the West Riding had 117 school clinics,[53] and 130 child welfare centres operating in 1939.[54]

The 1940s and '50s

During the 1940s and '50s Miss Wood continued working in Marsden and the Colne Valley. In Huddersfield the Milk Concession Scheme came into operation from 1 June 1940, when milk was supplied at 2d, 1d or free, to expectant and nursing mothers and children, depending on the net family income.[55] From 1 July 1940 the Ministry of Food Scheme for providing cheap, or, where necessary, free milk to expectant mothers and children under five, came into force.[56] Also the Welfare Food Service started and the Ministry of Food through their food offices, child health clinics, and other distribution points distributed National Dried Milk and vitamin supplements.[57]

Preventable disease was still prevalent and in 1943 several publications revealed many children were ill-fed and verminous. Poor health was often compounded with behavioural problems made worse by evacuation during the war.[58] The School Health Services recognized the importance of diet, claiming 10 per cent of schoolchildren were malnourished, and recommended a daily pint of milk.[59] National numbers of school nurses continued to increase before

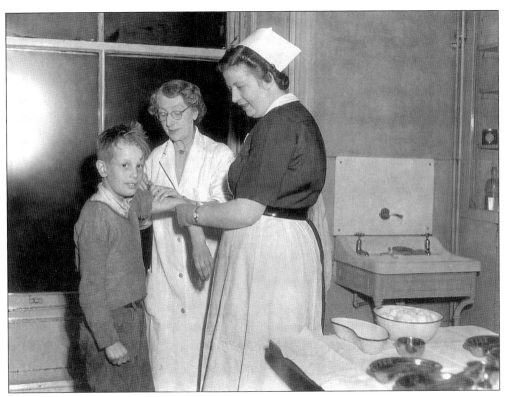

A nurse and a doctor vaccinating a schoolchild against polio, 1956. (Huddersfield Daily Examiner)

and after Miss Wood's retirement, rising from 2,366 in 1949 to 2,589 in 1959.[60]

By 1950 the national average infant mortality rate had reduced from 150 per 1,000 live births in 1900 to 29.7, with Child Welfare Nurses across the country playing their part in this.[61] At the end of food rationing in 1954, the Welfare Food Service transferred to the Ministry of Health and local health authorities undertook the distribution of welfare foods, other than liquid milk.[62] Poliomyelitis epidemics had taken eighteen lives in the Huddersfield area in 1949 and ten cases were reported in 1955.[63] In March parents waited for hours in queues to register their children for the newly developed vaccine, the first

delivery arriving in May 1956.[64] Infectious diseases that Miss Wood had seen throughout her career were still present.

Retirement

Miss Wood had a small, immediate family. Her parents lived in Woodhouse Hill and she nursed them until they died in the 1950s. She also had a sister who died of cancer when she was young.[65] Miss Wood retired on 30 September 1956, one of seventeen Health Visitors and School Nurses.[66] That year the Marsden Clinic held fifty-one child welfare sessions.[67] It was suggested that 'she knew the names of almost every one of the 3,000-plus children who came under her care during the twenty-seven years she worked in the

Miss Dorothy Wood on her ninetieth birthday.

Colne Valley.'[68] On retiring, she said 'I think I could remember their names if I met any of them. At one time I knew exactly when all their birthdays were.'[69] Newspaper reports illustrate her impact on Marsden. 'It's twenty-seven years ago that Nurse Wood walked down the steep streets into Marsden and won the hearts of the friendly people. She called them the friendly people. "I shall miss the friendly people terribly. But I shall come back and see them from time to time," she said yesterday.'[70] Upon her retirement she received a congratulatory letter from Colne Valley Urban District Council.[71]

She was a deeply religious person and in her later years a regular churchgoer at Christ Church near her home in Fartown. Her attendance gradually reduced due to her becoming crippled with arthritis.[72] She was said to have a 'strong community spirit'.[73]

Murder

At 0815hrs on 7 May 1996 Miss Wood, aged ninety-four, was found murdered at her home in Whitby Avenue, Fartown.[74] She had been smothered to death during a burglary. She was described as a ninety-four-year-old deaf, immobile woman, weighing just six stones.[75] Her friends, who found her dead, described how they communicated with her; they said she 'couldn't lip-read so we used to communicate to her by writing on notepaper.'[76] The police investigation offered a £5,000 reward.[77] During her murder investigation Detective Superintendent Haigh said 'It's so sad that such a good life should end in such a tragic way.'[78]

In August 1996 a Memorial Service was conducted at Woodhouse parish church.[79] A Memorial Bench near her Fartown home was provided in her memory.'[80] In 1999 the bench and plaque were restored after vandalism.[81]

She was cremated after a short service at Huddersfield Crematorium on 14 January 1998.[82] Her funeral was described as a 'moving Memorial Service for a 'lovable Christian lady' murdered in her bed.[83]

In December 1998 her murderer became the first person in the United Kingdom to be convicted of murder on the basis of an ear print found on a window of her home. 'Dorothy Wood dedicated her life to showing compassion and care for others. But she was shown no mercy at all by her killers.'[84]

The author would like to thank the following people for their help and advice in the preparation of this account: Mrs E.A. Hilary Haigh, Huddersfield University Archivist; staff of the West Yorkshire Archive Service at Wakefield, Kirklees and Calderdale; Stephen Carter, Manager of the Huddersfield Daily Examiner *Archive Library; and staff of the* Huddersfield Daily Examiner *photographic department.*

For end notes please see pp. 36-38.

Graham Thurgood

Colne Valley People and Working Men's Clubs

The room is a hive of activity; wall lights impart a softening glow on the tables arranged around the floor. Women and men smartly turned out for their Saturday evening's entertainment sit laughing,

The memorial plaque for Miss Wood. (Huddersfield Daily Examiner)

talking and waiting for the singer and her accompaniment to take to the stage. The barman and his helpers pull pints and beer flows readily. Committee members carry out their tasks – doors are manned, raffle tickets sold and bingo is called. A typical Saturday night in the local clubs. I look around with pride. Here the working man comes into his own: released from his working commitments, he organizes his club and leisure activities, and the evening proceeds smoothly; no worries about his bonus, short-time working or redundancies, the night is for pleasure and relaxation, the pints go down like milk.

I have always been aware of my working-class roots, and became more so through my studies at the Huddersfield Polytechnic. Harold Wilson and his Labour government had opened up education to the working classes in the 1970s and as an adult learner, I was accepted onto a course of study which gave me a totally new perspective on life through looking at social and psychological theories on the individual and society.

As an eleven-plus failure, I had passed through the Secondary Modern system of schooling, where the emphasis was placed on preparing the pupils for work in local industries and trade. We were well grounded in the three Rs and our school song defined our roles as workers in the valley, dedicated to honesty, thrift and vocation.

The textile industry in the Colne Valley was the main employer, with engineering a close runner-up in surrounding areas. We textile workers experienced periodic patches of 'short-time' working which generally occurred during the summer months – happily for teenagers, who didn't have to worry about household bills but who could enjoy a little freedom from the longish day worked at that time – there was always 'The Holidays at Home' programme in Greenhead park to keep us happy.

The mill hooter still sounded over the valley at 6.15 a.m. to rouse those dependent on the trade, just as it had done in my grandma's time. Grandma had to pass a special exam to leave school at the age of eleven so that she could look after a young child while her auntie worked, and at the age of thirteen started work as a weaver in a mill at Linthwaite.

The valley has held the sound of mill looms for more than a hundred years, and the people are of a hardy and tolerant stock, absorbing waves of immigrants arriving seeking work and sanctuary particularly after the Second World War. Many of them were from Eastern Europe, victims of fascism and devastation and not wishing to return to totalitarian regimes.

Woven into the valley lives, the Working Men's Clubs have played a significant role in arousing working-class consciousness. My father told me about the Hoyle Inge club at Linthwaite, which celebrated its centenary in 1979. One of the earliest in the valley, its members secretly paid one penny a week to the budding Labour movement. The Colne Valley Labour Union was set up on 21 July 1891 in the cellar of a cottage in Nab Lane, Slaithwaite, with an aim to form Labour Clubs in each district of the area to promote socialism.

During the Second World War, the valley's looms turned out khaki to clothe the Army; the stone cottages were blacked out each night to conceal them from enemy aircraft with their deadly cargoes; and the Home Guard was called out to duty when the sirens sounded, the searchlights over Manchester raking the skies to the west, clearly visible over the moor tops. Many of the valley's men fought: my own father was called to stand against the Japanese and gave five years of his life to the cause, through the jungles of Burma, the monsoons and the mud.

The war over, life returned to 'normal'! Memories abide of parents who worked to provide home and comforts for the growing family: a father working outdoors in all weathers, building houses, grafting with calloused hands; a mother, her war work ended, a working wife, with the discipline to running the home and bringing up a family. Looking back, I value my people, my valley, and most of all my freedom to think, speak and do, knowing that these rights have been fought for both in politics and in war, and should be guarded for ever.

Glenna Welsh

Crowlane Secondary Modern School pupils in 1950, rehearsing for a concert at Crowlane Youth Club, which was run each evening, Monday to Friday, in the school by dedicated teachers Mr Richard Grace and Mr Sydney Boothroyd.

End Notes

Richard Oastler: Champion of the Poor

[1] 'Slavery in Yorkshire', *Leeds Mercury*, 16 October 1830.

[2] Oastler to Daniel, 17 September 1832.

[3] *Parliamentary Papers, 1831-1832*, **xv**, pp. 454-455.

[4] *Huddersfield Examiner*, 9 March 1930.

[5] *Ibid.*

[6] *Ibid.* His wife was Mary Tatham, the daughter of a Nottingham lace manufacturer.

[7] A. Greenwood, *Richard Oastler: The Factory King* (Huddersfield, 1913), p. 4.

[8] Oastler became acquainted with the great William Wilberforce at this time.

[9] 'Mr Oastler's speech at Huddersfield', *Leeds Intelligencer*, 12 July 1832.

[10] R. Oastler, *Eternal Damnation to the Fiend-Begotten, Coarser Food New Poor Law* (London, 1837). The Act severely restricted access to outdoor relief and made help available through the brutally managed workhouses.

[11] *Huddersfield Examiner*, 10 May 1913. The Radicals met weekly at the Ship Inn, Huddersfield.

[12] C. Driver, *Tory Radical: The Life of Richard Oastler* (New York, 1946), p. 88. The delegation consisted of John Leech, James Brook, Samuel Glendinning, John Hanson, Joshua Hobson and Lawrence Pitkethly. Oastler's secretary, Samuel Kydd, wrote in 1858 that Pitkethly had 'from the first to the last... been to Mr Oastler as a right arm.' *Huddersfield Examiner*, 2 June 1958.

[13] F. Driver, 'Tory Radicalism? Ideology, Strategy and Locality in Popular Politics during the 1830s', *Northern History*, **xxvii** (1991), p. 122.

[14] R. Oastler, *Convocation: The Church and the People* (Haymarket, 1860).

[15] Greenwood, 1913, p. 11.

[16] The letter was published on 16 October 1830.

[17] J.T. Ward, 'Richard Oastler on Politics and Factory Reform, 1832-1833', *Northern History*, **xxiv** (1988), p. 124.

[18] *Huddersfield Examiner*, 10 May 1913.

[19] C. Driver, 1946, p. 39.

[20] *Huddersfield Examiner*, 10 May 1913.

[21] Wood donated somewhere in the region of £40,000.

[22] *The Brook*, **24** no. 98, p. 10.

[23] J.A. Hargreaves, '"A Metropolis of Discontent": Popular Protest in Huddersfield', in E.A.H. Haigh, *Huddersfield: A Most Handsome Town* (Huddersfield, 1992), p. 210.

[24] R. Oastler, *DISGUSTING Unfeeling Impudence!!! To the Swinish Multitude*, West Yorkshire Archive Service, Kirklees, ref. KC174/140.

[25] *The Brook*, **24** no. 98, p. 9.

[26] *Parliamentary Papers, 1831-1832*, **xv**, pp. 454-455.

[27] *Leeds Intelligencer*, 12 July 1832.

[28] Greenwood, 1913, p. 19.

[29] S. Chadwick, *The Factory King: The Life and Labours of Richard Oastler* (Kirkburton, 1944), p. 5.

[30] Driver, 1946, pp. 420-421.

[31] R. Oastler, *The Fleet Papers; Being Letters to Thomas Thornhill, Esq.* (London, 1841), p. 1.

[32] Letter to Pitkethly, dated 1 February 1844, KC 1040, 5/4-5/5.

[33] Chadwick, 1944, p. 15.

[34] *Ibid.*, p. 13. The Metropolitan Police had helped to quell opposition to the new Poor Law Act in Huddersfield.

[35] J. Gardiner & N. Wenbom, *The History Today Companion to British History* (London, 1995), p. 737.

[36] Former Prime Minister, born in Huddersfield.

A Quiet Man and a Poet

[1] Ken Edward Smith, 'Fred Brown: A Biographical Sketch', in *Yorkshire Dialect Society Transactions*, 1990, p. 20.

[2] *Ibid.*, p. 22.

[3] *The Muse Went Weaving* (Hub/YDS, 1972), poem 36.

[4] C. Madge & T. Harrisson, *Britain by Mass Observation* (Penguin, 1939), p. 227.

[5] V. Cunningham, *British Writers of the Thirties* (Oxford University Press, 1989), p. 338.

[6] See *Northern Review*, **1** (1947) no. 9 (Beacon Publications, Leeds).

[7] See the preface to *The Muse Went Weaving* (see note 3 above), inside cover.

[8] *The Muse Went Weaving*, poem 2.

Dorothy Wood

[1] *Nursing Illustrated*, 16 August 1940, p. 727. Courtesy fo the University of Huddersfield Archives and Special Collections.

[2] B.M. Barrows, *A County and its Health: A History of the Development of the West Riding Health Services, 1889-1974* (The Health Committee of the West Riding County Council, 1974), p. 75. West Yorkshire Archives, Wakefield.

[3] C. Parton, *Liberal Individualism and Infant Mortality: The Infant Welfare Movement in Huddersfield, 1900-1918* (MA thesis, Huddersfield University, 1981).

[4] C. Parton, 'Infant welfare movement in early 20th century Huddersfield', *Journal of Regional and Local Studies*, **3**, 2 (Winter 1983). Huddersfield Local Library, B362.7.

[5] H. Marland, 'A pioneer in infant welfare: the Huddersfield Scheme, 1903-1920', *Society for the Social History of Medicine*, 1993, 25-50.

[6] H. Marland, 'Lay and Medical Conceptions of Medical Charity during the Nineteenth Century. The Case of the Huddersfield General Dispensary and Infirmary', in J. Barry & C. Jones, *Medicine and Charity before the Welfare State* (1991).

[7] H. Marland, 'Health Care in Nineteenth Century Huddersfield', in E.A.H. Haigh (ed.), *Huddersfield: A Most Handsome Town* (1992), chap. 23, pp. 597-620. Huddersfield, Kirklees Cultural Services.

[8] Courtesy of Stephen Carter, Manager, *Huddersfield Daily Examiner* Archive Library.

[9] KC 853/1 Millhouse Higher Elementary School Easter Report of 1917, West Yorkshire Archive Service, Kirklees.

[10] KC 853/2 School Final Certificate, dated 4 June 1917, and a first-class pass in her School Exam, West Yorkshire Archive Service, Kirklees.

[11] KC 853/3 West Yorkshire Archive Service, Kirklees.

[12] *Ibid.*

[13] The School of Medicine allowed nurses to share lectures with Diploma in Public Health students, who then took the Royal Sanitary Institute examination and qualified as Health Visitors. In 1926, the student health visitors were formalized as full university students and a course was run every year. Ref. DEP/100 Departmental Records:

Department of Public Health Medicine, 1925-1990. Leeds University Archive.

[14] Her attendance on this health visiting course is confirmed by her name being on a list of students in the university. Ref. Student Statistics, Administration Records. Leeds University Archives.

[15] MISC: 493/10. The minute book of the Ladies' Committee of the Halifax King Edward VII Nursing Association 7 April 1925 to 2 February 1941. West Yorkshire Archive Service, Calderdale.

[16] MISC: 493/67. Halifax District Nursing Association 17th Annual Report, 31 March 1929, p. 4. West Yorkshire Archive Service, Calderdale.

[17] RD7-3/6/18. Institutions and Charitable Agencies of Halifax. Halifax Council of Social Welfare and the Rotary Club of Halifax, 32 Clare Road, 1929, p. 38. West Yorkshire Archive Service, Wakefield.

[18] MISC: 493/50-107. Halifax District Nursing Association records, 1911-1981. Annual Reports, 1924, 1925, 1926, 1928. West Yorkshire Archive Service, Calderdale.

[19] E.I. Pearson, *Marsden Through the Ages* (Marsden, 1984). Kirklees Local History Library.

[20] *Ibid*.

[21] 'A Source of Valuable Work: Marsden Nursing Association', *Colne Valley Guardian*, 13 January 1933. Kirklees Local History Library.

[22] KC 853/3. 'Golden Jubilee Year of Marsden Child Welfare Clinic Committee' (newspaper cutting). West Yorkshire Archive Service, Kirklees.

[23] RC/6/79. Child Welfare Sub-Committee Signed Minutes, 1929-32, 6 March 1929 (p. 25). West Yorkshire Archive Service, Wakefield.

[24] KC 853/4 Photograph album. West Yorkshire Archive Service, Kirklees.

[25] RC/6/80. Child Welfare Sub-Committee of the West Riding County Council Education and Public Health and Housing Committee, Signed Minutes 1933-35, p. 53. West Yorkshire Archive Service, Wakefield.

[26] B.M. Barrows, 1974, *op. cit.* p. 75.

[27] A. Hirst, *Huddersfield Daily Examiner*, 8 May 1996. Courtesy of *Huddersfield Daily Examiner* Archive Library.

[28] E.I. Marsden, 1984, *op. cit.* p. 43.

[29] KC 853/3. West Yorkshire Archive Service, Kirklees.

[30] KC 853/5. Undated newspaper cutting. West Yorkshire Archive Service, Kirklees.

[31] Royal College of Nursing Education Committee Minutes, 1932, pp. 142i, 147b, 153h. RCN Archives, Edinburgh.

[32] KC 853/5. Undated newspaper cutting. West Yorkshire Archive Service, Kirklees.

[33] RC/6/79. Child Welfare Sub-Committee Signed Minutes, 1929-32, 13 July 1932 (p. 422). West Yorkshire Archive Service, Wakefield.

[34] RC/6/80. Child Welfare Sub-Committee of the West Riding County Council Education and Public Health and Housing Committee, Signed Minutes 1933-35, 12 April 1933 (pp. 27-8). West Yorkshire Archive Service, Wakefield.

[35] Editorial, *Nursing Times*, 27 August 1932, p. 878. Courtesy of the RCN Archives, Edinburgh.

[36] *Ibid*.

[37] RC/6/79. Child Welfare Sub-Committee Signed Minutes, 1929-32, 5 March 1930 (p. 143). West Yorkshire Archive Service, Wakefield.

[38] KC 853/5. Undated newspaper cutting. West Yorkshire Archive Service, Kirklees.

[39] Royal College of Nursing Education Committee Minutes, 1933. RCN Archives, Edinburgh.

[40] KC 853/5. Undated newspaper cutting. West Yorkshire Archive Service, Kirklees.

[41] KC 853/3 & 853/5. Newspaper cuttings. West Yorkshire Archive Service, Kirklees.

[42] KC 853/3. Newspaper cutting: '"Toxoid Gospel to be spread." Yorkshire Nurse to Recommend Toronto System in England' (undated). West Yorkshire Archive Service, Kirklees.

[43] D. Wood, 'A Scholarship Holder Goes to Canada', *Nursing Times*, 4 February 1933, p. 104. Courtesy of RCN Archives, Edinburgh.

[44] D. Wood, 'News from Canada', *Nursing Times*, 29 April 1933, p. 425. Courtesy of RCN Archives, Edinburgh.

[45] KC 853/5. West Yorkshire Archive Service, Kirklees.

[46] Royal College of Nursing Education Committee Minutes, 1933, pp. 1294,8 & 200,8. RCN Archives, Edinburgh.

[47] Royal College of Nursing Education Committee Minutes, 1933, p. 181d. RCN Archives, Edinburgh.

[48] RC/6/80. Child Welfare Sub-Committee of the West Riding County Council Education and Public Health and Housing Committee, Signed Minutes 1933-35. West Yorkshire Archive Service, Wakefield.

[49] *Colne Valley Almanack 1936-9*, p. 76. Kirklees Local History Library, K900.

[50] *Huddersfield Weekly Examiner*, 24 September 1932. West Yorkshire Archive Service, Kirklees.

[51] 'The Diphtheria Epidemic', *Huddersfield Weekly Examiner*, 25 Novemmber 1933. West Yorkshire Archive Service, Kirklees.

[52] 'Inoculation against Diphtheria', *Colne Valley Guardian*, 22 December 1933. West Yorkshire Archive Service, Kirklees.

[53] B.J. Barber & M.W. Beresford, *The West Riding County Council, 1889-1974: Historical Studies*, Wakefield, West Yorkshire Metropolitan County Council, 1979, p. 52. West Yorkshire Archive Service, Wakefield.

[54] *Ibid.*, p. 57.

[55] *Nursing Illustrated*, 31 May 1940, p. 402. Courtesy of the University of Huddersfield Archives and Special Collections.

[56] *Nursing Illustrated*, 1 July 1940, p. 557. Courtesy of the University of Huddersfield Archives and Special Collections.

[57] HMSO, *Child Welfare Centres*, 1967, p. 22. Central Health Services Council, Standing Medical Advisory Committee, DHSS, London.

[58] M.E. Baly, *Nursing and Social Change*, 3rd ed. (London, Heinemann Medical Books, 1995), pp. 242-4.

[59] *Nursing Illustrated*, 29 March 1940, p. 108. Courtesy of the University of Huddersfield Archives and Special Collections.

[60] M.E. Baly, 1995, *op. cit.* Appendix 7c.

[61] HMSO, 1967, *op. cit.* p. 7.

[62] *Ibid.*, p. 22.

[63] *Images of Huddersfield* (Breedon Books, 1994), p. 149.

[64] *Ibid.*

[65] A. Hirst, *Huddersfield Daily Examiner*, 8 May 1996. Courtesy of Huddersfield Archive Library.

[66] WF C381/11/11. E. Ward, *Urban District of Meltham – A Report*, 1956, p. 2a. West Yorkshire Archive Service, Wakefield.

[67] *Ibid.*, p. 19a.

[68] A. Hirst, *Huddersfield Daily Examiner*, 7 May 1997. Courtesy of *Huddersfield Daily Examiner* Archive Library.

[69] A. Hirst, 'Friendly people say goodbye', *Huddersfield Daily Examiner*, 8 May 1996. Courtesy of *Huddersfield Daily Examiner* Archive Library.

[70] KC 853/5. Newspaper cutting. West Yorkshire Archive Service, Kirklees.

[71] KC 853/3. Official letter dated 23 November 1956. West Yorkshire Archive Service, Kirklees.

[72] N. Atkinson, A. Hirst, *Huddersfield Daily Examiner*, 15 December 1998, 1 January 1999. Courtesy of *Huddersfield Daily Examiner* Archive Library.

[73] A. Hirst, *Huddersfield Daily Examiner*, 7 May 1997. Courtesy of *Huddersfield Daily Examiner* Archive Library.

[74] KC 853/5 *Huddersfield Daily Examiner* cutting, 7 May 1997. Courtesy of *Huddersfield Daily Examiner* Archive Library.

[75] L. Greer, 'The Dorothy Wood Case', *Police Review*, 5 November 1999, pp. 29-30. Courtesy of *Huddersfield Daily Examiner* Archive Library.

[76] A. Hirst, *Huddersfield Daily Examiner*, 9 May 1996. Courtesy of *Huddersfield Daily Examiner* Archive Library.

[77] KC 853/5. Newspaper cutting. West Yorkshire Archive Service, Kirklees.

[78] A. Hirst, *Huddersfield Daily Examiner*, 9 May 1996. Courtesy of *Huddersfield Daily Examiner* Archive Library.

[79] KC 853/5. Newspaper cutting, 23 August 1996. West Yorkshire Archive Service, Kirklees.

[80] A. Hirst, *Huddersfield Daily Examiner*, 7 May 1997. Courtesy of *Huddersfield Daily Examiner* Archive Library.

[81] *Huddersfield Daily Examiner*, 16 November 1999. Courtesy of *Huddersfield Daily Examiner* Archive Library.

[82] Courtesy of *Huddersfield Daily Examiner* Archive Library.

[83] A. Hirst, *Huddersfield Daily Examiner*, 28 August 1996. Courtesy of *Huddersfield Daily Examiner* Archive Library.

[84] A. Hirst, *Huddersfield Daily Examiner*, 7 May 1997. Courtesy of *Huddersfield Daily Examiner* Archive Library.

Robin Hood's Grave and Kirklees Priory Gatehouse at Hartshead, near Brighouse, West Yorkshire.

The Mystery of Robin Hood's Grave

Deep in the heart of an ancient woodland in West Yorkshire, beneath a formidable barrier of fierce thorns and dense undergrowth, there is a hidden grave. Here rest the mortal remains of Robin Hood, the Prince of Robbers, England's outlaw hero, bloodily slain by the Prioress of Kirklees Nunnery 600 years ago and cast into an unhallowed grave. Today, Robin lies forgotten and unmourned in his lonely and desolate sepulchre, for few people know of the grave's existence or its whereabouts. Why is this so? Should not such a monument be an international place of pilgrimage and Yorkshire, not Nottingham, be the centre of the famous folk hero's legend? A mystery indeed which this short article attempts to unravel a little. We will begin with the strange death of Robin Hood.

The Death of Robin Hood

Shee laid the blood irons to Robin Hood's vain
Alacke the more pitye!
And perct the vaine and let out the bloode
That was full red to see,
At first it bled the thicke thicke blood
And afterwards the thinne,
And well then wist good Robin Hood
Treason there was within.
Robin Hood His Death and Burial, vv. 16-17.

The circumstances of Robin Hood's death are fairly well known. Realising he is dying, Robin decides to be bled by his kinswoman, the prioress of Kirklees, a woman 'skilled in physic'. Will Scarlet is against this, but Robin sets out on the journey accompanied by his faithful comrade in arms, Little John. On the way to the priory, they meet an old hag by a stream who 'bans' (curses) Robin for reasons unknown, some of the manuscript page being unfortunately missing:

They came to blacke water
And over it laid a plank.
Upon it kneeled an old woman
Was banning Robin Hood.
Robin Hood His Death and Burial, vv. 8-9.

On arrival at the nunnery, the prioress takes Robin into the gatehouse and sends Little John away. She then proceeds to bleed Robin, accompanied by her lover, the convent priest 'Red Roger of Doncaster', however, she bled him to death. When he realizes he is dying, Robin summons Little John to his assistance by blowing three blasts on his hunting horn. When Little John arrives it is too late to save Robin, but he helps his beloved leader fire his last arrow from the gatehouse window, promising Robin that he will bury him where it falls. Little John vows to raze the nunnery to the ground and put all the nuns to the sword in revenge for the prioress's vile deed, but Robin forbids him, reminding his distraught friend that it was their code never to hurt women.

Robin's grave, 600 yards from the gatehouse – thought to be an improbable arrow shot for a dying man – is, today, neglected and overgrown and enclosed in rusted, twisted iron railings, erected in Victorian times. The inscription, in pseudo-Gothic, reads:

HERE UNDERNEATH DIS LAITL STEAN
LAZ ROBERT EARL OF HUNTINGTUN
NE'ER ARCIR VER AS HIE SA GEUD
AN PIPL KAULD IM ROBIN HEUD
SICK UTLAWZ AS HIS AN IZ MEN
VIL ENGLAND NIVR SI AGEN

Bossy Bishops and Naughty Nuns

Kirklees Priory was founded in the twelfth century by Reinor de Fleming, manor lord of Clifton, near Brighouse. The Rule was Cistercian and at first was very strict, but as time passed the 'White Ladies', so called because of the colour of their undyed woollen habits, became less dedicated to the religious ideal. Many of them were the unwanted daughters of gentry with no real vocation to the cloistered life. The sisters were often admonished by visiting bishops for indulging in worldly ways, keeping dogs, trimming their habits with brooches and furs, going out dancing, and for inviting men onto the holy premises!

In 1300 Pope Boniface VIII published a Papal Bull, *Periculoso*, which forbade such unseemly goings-on, but the nuns at the convent to which it was delivered threw the document after the unfortunate bishop who came to deliver it and chased him off the premises. In 1315 there were scandalous reports in circulation about the nuns of Kirklees. It was reported that one 'Alice de Raggid, deceived by the allurements of frail flesh, in great levity of mind, hath gone forth from her house and hath wandered, in great peril, having long ago put off her religious habit.' Later, two more nuns, Elizabeth de Hopton and Joan de Heton, along with the rebellious Alice (who must have returned to the nunnery by then) were accused of admitting both clergy and laymen to the 'secret places of the monastery ... from which there is suspicion of sin and great scandal arises.' No wonder Robin came to a sticky end among such flighty creatures!

The nunnery was finally dissolved, along with other Yorkshire monasteries, by Henry VIII in 1539, after which Kirklees Hall was built on the nearby hillside, using the stones of the fallen priory. Only the gatehouse, where Robin died, was left standing. Today, like the grave, it is in danger of being lost to our heritage as it slowly crumbles away, unchecked and unhindered by any official attempts to prevent the destruction.

The Riddle of the Prioress

Who then, was the wicked prioress who bled Robin Hood to death? The only prioress's grave still to be seen at Kirklees is that of Elizabeth de Staynton (or Stainton) but there is no date on her tombstone. The Reverend Harold Pobjoy, Vicar of Hartshead in the 1930s and a historian who wrote *A History of the Ancient Parish of Hartshead-cum-Clifton*, gives a list of prioresses taken from Dugdale's *Monasticum*. He also quotes from Hopkirk's *Huddersfield, its History and Natural History* from 1846 which has a similar list, but unfortunately Hopkirk does not name his sources. The two lists can be slotted together without causing any discrepancy, although there are gaps. The problem of the prioress's identity is further compounded by the fact that no one knows for certain the date of Robin's death, but research suggests it may have been 1347. The reasons for this are based on the theory that Robin was a Wakefield man, outlawed in 1322 at the Battle of Boroughbridge. He was pardoned and then spent around eighteen months at the court of Edward II, his name being mentioned in the Court Rolls of that king for 1323-1324, after which he returned to the greenwood for a further twenty-two years, bringing the date to 1347. This date is exactly 100 years later than that on Robin's Victorian tombstone, and the latter could be a miscopying of the original. If 1347 is the true date of his death, then the prioress in question was Dame Mary Startin, not Elizabeth de Staynton. According to Eileen Power in her book *Medieval English Nunneries* (Cambridge University Press), Dame Mary died in 1350 during the Black Death, although some ballads say that the prioress committed suicide after murdering Robin.

Elizabeth de Staynton, on the other hand, could not have been prioress in 1347. She was one of the four daughters of John de Staynton of Woolley near Wakefield. Following her father's death, Elizabeth's

Ye Olde Kirklees Sign

Kirklees Priory Gatehouse (top right), Robin Hood's Grave and the Prioress's Grave in the grounds of Kirklees Hall.

There is mention of a woman called Matilda in the Wakefield Court Rolls of 1314 being arrested for stealing the lord's firewood.

They assume that this Matilda became Robin's wife and Elizabeth's sister in law, but do not explain why Elizabeth went on to murder him in later years. If this hypothesis is correct, however, we might consider a lethal love triangle here, Robin falling in love with Matilda, while Elizabeth was packed off to the nunnery suffering from a medieval 'fatal attraction' – exacting her revenge for her thwarted passion in later years! However, as we have seen, the dates do not fit – this scenario is thirty years too early. Another mysterious clue lies in a document quoted by Wakefield historian J.W. Walker. This is also mentioned by Pobjoy, who reports a dispute over eighteen acres of land between 'the prioress of Kirklees and Esmon, son of the noble Richard of England and the Earl of Kent, in 1373.' The medieval Latin text reads: '1373, Orate pro Elizabetha de Staynton quondam prioressa Kirklees quo intempere illus du carta fuit adquista' and translates: 'Pray for Elizabeth de Staynton formerly prioress of Kirklees at which time the document was acquired.' This seems to suggest that Elizabeth was prioress prior to 1373 but it can be read either way. J.W. Walker also quotes another document which he states says the prioress of Kirklees (he infers Elizabeth) signed a legal document in 1348, but the British Library have been unable to verify the entry which was not under the reference quoted (Harleian 4360 Folio 517) so the riddle still remains.

Finally, why did the prioress kill Robin? Venesection, or 'bleeding', was a common medical practice in the Middle Ages. Many people must have died as a result, but it was an ignominious end for the swashbuckling

mother married Hugh de Toothill in 1344 and Elizabeth and her sister were sent to be nuns at Kirklees for reasons of family economy. William de Notton, her uncle and guardian, took provision that the girls had not been forced into the religious life, and a document was signed at Monk Bretton Priory in 1347, protecting the interests of Elizabeth and her sister (from a deed at Wooley Hall in the possession of Lt-Cmdr Wentworth). Graham Collins and Martin Keatman in their book *Robin Hood: The Man Behind the Myth* (1995) have a theory about Elizabeth which connects her with Robert and Matilda Hood of Wakefield. They suggest that when Elizabeth's mother married Hugh de Toothill, his daughter by his first wife, called Matilda, married Robin.

Robin, whether by accident or design. The ballads state that the prioress and her lover 'Red Roger of Doncaster' murdered Robin in revenge for his opposition to the corruption in the Church. If it was murder – for whatever reason – it was a particular treacherous and gruesome act. It has even been suggested that, in the symbolic spilling of his blood, Robin's death could have been linked with pagan sacrifice, vampirism, or Christ's death on the cross. There is a fascinating mystery here, still waiting to be solved, but until all the evidence is uncovered this part of Robin's legend will remain shrouded in darkness and is one of Yorkshire's buried treasure, in more ways than one.

The Haunting of Robin Hood's Grave

'The Armytage family lived over the brow of the hill on a splendid site once occupied by Cistercian nuns. It was called Kirklees. There was more than an insularity which set the mansion apart. There was a mystery about it which local people only reluctantly tried to penetrate. The mystery was helped physically by the thick shroud of trees that surrounded the place and was sustained by local tales of ghosts of prioresses and nuns and or the death of Robin Hood whose grave is so imperturbably marked as lying within Kirklees grounds in spite of any facts which might suggest to the contrary.' (*The Land of Lost Content*)

This would appear to be the first reported mention of ghostly activity around Robin Hood's Grave, but considering the history of Robin's death cursed by a witch on his way to the nunnery, murdered by an apostate nun and cast into an unhallowed grave, it is hardly surprising that the site is reputed to have unquiet spirits hovering around. An elderly lady, Mrs Edith Ellis, witnessed silver arrows in the sky above Kirklees when visiting her old aunt at Hartshead in the early years of the last century. She also reports hearing Robin calling for Marian.

Another sighting was made by a tenant farmer of Kirklees in 1926. 'One day,' he recalls, 'I was sitting on the grave shooting rabbits. As I was about to shoot I felt a tap on my shoulder, and my shotgun went off accidentally, removing two of my front teeth with its recoil. There was nobody to be seen at the time. On another occasion I was on my way home from the Three Nuns. As I was walking through the woods something fell out of a tree and knocked me to the ground. When I got up I could see the old gatehouse. In the window I could clearly see a man with a bow. My family always said it was the drink, but it was Robin Hood's ghost.'

In 1963 guitarist Roger Williams took an unofficial stroll up to Robin's grave with a friend. About twenty yards from the grave he saw a white-robed woman who suddenly seemed to glide towards the two men. What made Roger's hair stand on end was how silently she moved over the twigs and bracken. At about five yards from Roger the woman stopped and stared at him with 'dark, mad eyes'. Then she moved away and vanished. It was 2.30 p.m. on a bright sunny day. Roger Williams saw the same apparition again in 1972, in full daylight, and again she stopped a few yards from him and his companion. This time Roger remembered a few more details. The woman was wearing a long white dress with a square neck and long sleeves which accords with the habit of a Cistercian nun. Again she looked at him angrily before moving off, but the eerie sequel to this experience was that Roger's house then experienced a series of strange noises and bangings. After this, Roger swore that 'wild horses would not drag me up there again.'

Mark Gibbons, one of the founder members of Gravewatch, had a similar experience in 1998. With other members of the group he had gone up to try and find Robin's grave one moonlit night, but they had got lost. Suddenly Mark saw a white figure pointing in a certain direction—which turned out to be where the grave was situated. Mark also experienced a sensation of great evil and hatred.

Shortly after this Judith Broadbent, a journalist from the *Dewsbury Reporter*, and a photographer colleague, Sue Ellis, were allowed to visit the grave site by the owner. While wandering around she heard heavy footsteps behind her and she was pulled to the ground by invisible forces. She shouted 'get away' and her friend came rushing to help her. Her camera had jammed while trying to photograph the grave. A week later Sue was taken seriously ill and was paralysed from the neck downwards for two weeks. The two reporters later wrote their experiences up for *Yorkshire Life* magazine, much of its content being taken from Yorkshire Robin Hood Society literature, including the next sighting, which appeared in *The Unexplained* magazine in 1992, prior to the publication of their article.

This was when vampires entered the arena, introduced to the increasing enigmatic situation by Bishop Sean Manchester of the Holy Grail Church and patron of the Yorkshire Robin Hood Society. In 1992 Bishop Manchester and two colleagues attempted an exorcism at Kirklees. This had come about as a result of the Yorkshire Robin Hood Society asking for the site to be blessed by the local vicar, Father John Flack. Unfortunately permission to perform such a ceremony had been unequivocally refused to both clergymen. Bishop Manchester, however, was made of sterner stuff than the local pastor! He was renowned for his involvement in the notorious Highgate Vampire affair in the 1970s and it occurred to him that vampires might be behind the legend of Robin being bled to death and this needed urgent spiritual intervention. He was the man for the job, with or without official sanction! Suffice to say that on his clandestine visit to the grave the bishop came across the body of a blood drained goat, diabolical rune signs on the priory gatehouse and finger-width holes in the ground round the grave, all suggesting vampiric activity. He was then confronted by a darkly clad woman who turned into a hag with red staring eyes.

My own experience was something like a panic attack beside the grave, when I saw two figures hovering in the trees, one whom I took to be the prioress and the other Red Roger of Doncaster. I felt, and saw, what I can only describe as streams of evil pouring out of the trees towards me. Other visitors, including Vi Jones of Nottingham, who visited the grave in the summer of 2000, experienced a psychic communication with Robin at the graveside, as did John Pope de Locksley of the London Robin Hood Club, who also boldly battled through the giant ferns, murderous brambles and other lethal obstacles of the Kirklees rainforest to stand by his hero's grave one wild, wet October night the same year!

It is true that Robin's grave was excavated in an amateurish way by a Victorian Armytage and the ground beneath found to be undisturbed, but the many historical documents naming Kirklees as Robin's final resting place cannot be ignored. The fact is, his bones could lie anywhere on that hillside, while a gravestone resembling the original one drawn by Dr Johnstone, is to be found in the nearby Hartshead churchyard to where it may have been moved during the Civil War.

Many visitors to the grave have recorded their experiences for posterity, including the following quotation from a Victorian tourist: 'I had the strangest emotions when I first stood over the grave of this old forest hero. I stood there and had no words, nor can I find any now to tell what my feelings were, Bravehearted Robin! Thou hast found a fit resting place in this glorious park, among these solemn yews and silent trees.'

A hundred years later it is a different story: 'There it was, looming out of the dark, a massive, broken edifice, a huge ship of stone, wrecked in the everglades of Kirklees. Fallen pillars and twisted railings were were all that remained of Yorkshire's buried treasure. We had found Robin Hood's Grave.' (Mark Gibbons, *Secrets of the Grave*)

Maybe the last word should be with Victorian poet, George Searle Phillips, a friend of the Brontës, who visited the grave in 1848, and wrote an epic poem, a small section of which is quoted here:

Tread lightly o'er the earth and speak no word
Till the Great Spirit doth unloose your tongues
For where those yew trees nod their funereal
plumes
Upon the highest platform of the hill,
Lies gentle Robin Hood, his mighty heart
All muffled up in dust and his bright eyes
Quenched in eternal darkness. Never more
Shall the woods echo to his bugle horn,
Or his unerring arrow strike the deer
Swift flying, till it hits the bloody grass.

Barbara Green

Holy Smoke? Fire on Castle Hill

It's June; but it's cold and damp in the low cloud that shrouds the high ground above Almondbury. The elements are in tune with the metaphoric veil of mystery that hangs over the ancient earthworks. Suddenly the mist is pierced by a stone edifice. Like a giant exclamation mark added for effect, Victoria's tower proclaims the pre-eminence of our natural landmark: Castle Hill.

Thousands of years ago Stone Age people – hunter-gatherers, early farmers – emerged from the surrounding swamps and forests to gaze up at the hill and, for a time, they made it their home. Down through the ages others were drawn here; some lived in peace while others had to defend themselves behind protective walls. By the middle of the fifth century BC the thatched round-houses of the folk who lived on the hill were enclosed by a series of ramparts and ditches: these folk intended to stay. Today we are still drawn by the hill's unique magnetism. For those of us who live beneath the old ramparts, Castle Hill has become part of our collective consciousness. Little wonder that over the centuries myths and legends have evolved around this special place.

In the age of Elizabeth I, William Camden reported that the hill had been a Roman fort, the seat of an Anglo-Saxon king and the site of a cathedral founded by the Christian missionary Paulinus. Legends relate to a visitation by the Devil, secret subterranean passages, a golden cradle, buried treasure and, of course, a dragon. Eminent historians and archaeologists believed that in Roman times Castle Hill was the stronghold of Cartimandua, Queen of the Brigantes – a loose confederacy of Celtic tribes inhabiting most of the north of Britain at the time of the Roman Conquest.

Castle Hill

Pro-Roman Cartimandua is notorious for betraying the fugitive British resistance leader Caratacus in AD 51. For this act of treachery, she was well rewarded with luxury goods from the Empire. But to date the spade has failed to unearth any rich Roman artefacts, any remains of an Anglo-Saxon royal household, or any sign of Christian worship.

Excavations carried out intermittently between 1939 and 1972 suggested that the hill's first occupancy dates from the third millennium BC. Around 600 BC Iron Age settlers built a simple hill fort which was modified down the years, becoming more and more sophisticated over the next century and a half, until catastrophe struck and the fort was destroyed by fire. It would appear that the hill was then deserted until the Norman de Laci family built a castle on the south-west elevation (where the Jubilee Tower now stands) in the twelfth century. A climb to the summit of Castle Hill reveals the site's strategic importance. Why should a site of such obvious advantage have remained unused for so many hundreds of years?

In the absence of hard archaeological evidence, myths and legends may hold the key to the secrets of our mysterious mound. Local folklore should not be dismissed as mere old wives' tales: legends of the Devil often indicate important religious significance and point to a site's pagan past. Just outside Aldborough, for example, on the road to Boroughbridge, there are three massive stones called the Devil's Arrows. Local legend says they were cross-bow bolts fired at an early Christian missionary settlement. These 'Devil's arrows' are standing stones erected by the folk who were a mystery even to the Celts. The area around Rudston in the Yorkshire Wolds was also a sacred pagan centre. Near the village church stands a massive monolith that once dominated the Stone Age landscape. According to Christian legend, it was a missile hurled by the Devil at the village church. Fortunately, he missed his target.

Such legends are a folk-memory of the demonizing of the old gods once honoured there. Proponents of the new religion would often Christianize a sacred pagan place by building a church on the site. Rudston is a good example; Brigit, goddess of fire and the hearth, was worshipped here for centuries by the people whom the Romans called 'Brigantes': people of the goddess Brigit, 'the exalted one'. Is it possible that Castle Hill could have been such a place? The folklore certainly suggest that this might be so.

In late medieval times Castle Hill was

known as Wormecliffe. The name may originate in the Old English *wyrm* which meant 'dragon', or perhaps it derives from the Norse word for serpent, *ormr*. Vikings certainly lived near by because they have left evidence in the place-name Scale Hill: *skal* is the Norse word for a rough shelter used by people tending cattle on high ground. In myth and legend the dragon and serpent are often synonymous. Northumbria has several dragon legends, notably that of the Lambton Worm. The name 'Wormecliffe' is strongly suggestive of a dragon story, but it appears to have been lost. Dragons often guard treasure; could the lost legend have been linked to a golden cradle?

In pre-Christian times the dragon/serpent was a benign emblem. Classically-inspired representations of Brigit, and many other ancient goddesses, are often entwined with serpents. In Celtic myth they symbolized potent forces of the land: all energy, life, power and death were thought to come from beneath the ground and were ruled over by a goddess. This concept was related to the fate of the land and its inhabitants; Wales still uses the red dragon as a national emblem. Serpents are also associated with healing. However, the Book of Revelation identifies the dragon directly with 'that old serpent, called the Devil' (12:9). Our lost dragon story may have merged, at some point in time, with that of Old Nick who, after hurling himself out of Hell and bouncing around the area, is said to have landed finally on Castle Hill. Unfortunately he disappeared down one of the legendary underground passages and ended up back in his fiery abode.

Tales of dragons, serpents and the Devil, links to the underworld, evidence of a great conflagration: could Brigit, tutelary goddess of the Brigantes, hold the key? Brigit, Brigan, Brigantia, Brighid, Bride: there are many variations of her name. She had many functions; she ruled over the hearth fire, she was patroness of smithcraft, poetry, fertility and childbirth, and is said to have inspired the alphabet. An altar found at Greetland in 1597 is dedicated to Brigantia as goddess of victory; a stone relief found at Birrens, the Roman military site in Dumfriesshire, depicts Brigantia holding a spear and a globe of victory. The conquerors often assimilated native deities into the own pantheon; it was good PR. Brigantia at Birrens shared some of the attributes of the Roman Minerva. But the Celts often referred to her as a triple goddess of wisdom, healing and fire; as such, her attribute was the serpent.

So well-loved was Brigit by the Celtic people that she avoided demonization by the Church and was Christianized; she became Saint Bridget, or Bride. In the Hebrides, St Bride was held to be the midwife at the birth of Christ; perhaps there is a link here with a 'golden cradle'? Her feast day is 1 February, the old pagan spring festival of Imbolc. Nuns kept a sacred flame burning at her abbey in Kildare, Ireland, up until the Reformation; no man was allowed anywhere near. This is reminiscent of the holy fire tended by the Virgins of Vesta, the Roman fire goddesses worshipped by women at the hearth, and probably represents the continuation into Christian times of a pagan rite. Brigit, as both saint and goddess, is patroness of the hearth, the earthly counterpart of the sun's heavenly fire.

Fire symbolism relates to the saint's early life: as a child her home caught fire as she lay sleeping. But this was a magical fire: the house, like Moses' bush, burned but was not consumed and the occupants emerged unscathed. Could Castle Hill, thought for so long to be a 'stronghold of the Brigantes' have been another site sacred to Brigit, goddess of fire?

Evidence of the great fire that destroyed the hill fort at Almondbury was as obvious to the archaeologists, when they began digging in 1939, as it would have been to William Camden. It showed quite clearly, particularly on the south and west sides of the hill. Was it the result of attack by a hostile Celtic tribe or was it systematic destruction on the part of the Romans? Had it, as Camden believed, been fired during the wars between the British and the Anglo-Saxons? The archaeologists were about to find out that this had been no ordinary fire. The burning of Castle Hill was not contrived by human agency.

Some sections of the ramparts had burned so intensely as to reduce their timber core to charcoal, while other sections close by were hardly affected. In some instances the stones either side of the destroyed core were not burnt at all. Science would unlock at least some of the hill's mysteries. In the latter stages of the dig, experts from the National Coal Board and the Physics Department of Huddersfield Polytechnic were called in to help explain the phenomenon. Tests revealed that the source of heat lay in or near the timbers which formed the core of the rampart. The combined expertise of the archaeologists, the NCB and the Polytechnic reached the conclusion that the likeliest source of such intense heat had to be spontaneous combustion.

To the ancestors of the Brigantes, the destruction of their fort must have been a catastrophe indeed, after the years of toil it had taken to build their sophisticated system of defences. And yet, when the heat had died down sufficiently for them to climb up and inspect the smoking ruins, they would have found their roundhouses still intact behind the blackened walls. The stones of their homes and hearths were untouched by the fiery serpent unleashed from the bowels of the earth. Truly, this must have seemed like fire from heaven.

Radio carbon tests dated the fire on Castle Hill to around 431 BC. Despite the devastation the archaeologists found no sign of burning in the shelters which lie behind the ramparts. Neither did they find any evidence that the occupants made any attempt to repair their defences. Excavations on a total of forty sections revealed that none had been repaired; perhaps the occupants had been content to live without defences, but it seems unlikely. The archaeological survey, begun in 1939 and finally completed in 1972, suggested that by the time the Romans arrived in our area, the hill fort was a deserted ruin, that it lay undisturbed throughout the Anglo-Saxon period and was not disturbed again until the thoroughly Christianized Normans built their castle over the ruins in the twelfth century.

Did the hill acquire a taboo? The flames must have been visible for miles around; these highly superstitious folk had witnessed a manifestation of the fire goddess. The patroness of hearths had spared their homes, but to rebuild the walls would have been sacrilege since the ruins were her sacred handiwork. Romans, Saxons, Vikings, all had the greatest respect for a fire goddess and would never risk her wrath.

This is all conjecture, of course. But myths and legends surely contain some element of truth; they are created by way of explanation for events not readily understood. However there was no tangible evidence to suggest that Castle Hill became a sacred site. And the theories linking the hill to Cartimandua, the Anglo-Saxon king, and the cathedral built by Paulinus were, apparently, shot down in flames. But Dr R.J. Varley, the archaeologist who carried out the excavations, wrote in the introduction to his Report: 'Naturally, there is always more which could be done and better done, but as archaeology has still a lot more to learn, it would be sensible to wait until the new learning comes along after the customary respectful interval.'

The respectful interval elapsed, the new learning came along. In the final years of the twentieth century high-tech electronic equipment revealed, without recourse to the spade, structures hidden from Dr Varley and his team: evidence of a medieval building, more evidence of Stone Age occupation, 'hints' of Roman occupancy, traces of the Vikings... In the absence of more solid evidence speculation has free rein.

Since the Insular Celts were not in the habit of building shrines to their gods and goddesses – at least not until they came under Roman influence – archaeology may never be able to prove one way or the other that Castle Hill was a sacred site. The Celts worshipped in the open air, near wells and streams, and in groves; they left offerings and they made sacrifices to their gods. One of the wells excavated by Dr Varley was found to be full of animal remains, but these were not sacrifices. The fact that the de Laci's castle was eventually down-graded to a mere hunting lodge provides an explanation for the remains of birds and beasts of all kinds present in the well shaft. But another well,

discovered while digging out the foundations of the Jubilee Tower in 1897, was never properly excavated.

Will science provide us with another chance to probe the well for votive offerings without disturbing the tower? Will the Roman occupancy hinted at by the geophysicists turn out to be a look-out station, or will it be a shrine to Dea Brigantia? Is there still the possibility of unearthing a Christian church built, perhaps, to defuse the power of the old gods?

We are at the beginning of a new millennium. As I write, Castle Hill is about to embark on a new phase; action is needed to protect it from the damage caused by its own power to attract. The future of the hill is under debate: council and community will have their say regarding its fate. But beware of the dragon. A series of accidents that befell some of those involved in the construction of the Jubilee Tower suggests to the superstitious that the 'old gods' were angered by the disturbance. Perhaps there were similar manifestations of their anger when the Normans arrived, and again, early in the nineteenth century when the Hotel was built.

Defended only by the hostile gorse, itself under threat, Castle Hill is once again at the mercy of potent forces. Should we let sleeping dragons lie?

Maureen Whitehead

Bradley's Early Days

The history of the area known today as Bradley is far from complete and it is not the easiest of villages to research. It has a rather chequered history, some of which can be traced through legend more than through the history books. Looking at the names of many of the roads that we have on the estate built in the 1950s will give you some indication of this history: for instance Priory Place, Friar Place and Oak Road. Some of these roads have very legendary and picturesque names, some of them indicate that they may have been derived from other parts of the country, such as Sherwood Avenue and Huntingdon Avenue. There is also a public house called the Little John situated in the centre of the estate. But the people who now live in Bradley have a feeling that Bradley really is a place of beauty and growth. Keldregate, another of the roads in Bradley could have possibly taken its name from the Keldre, which from an early report is the name given to the River Calder.

The village had religious links to monasteries such as the Fountains Abbey estate. The monks there were responsible for the upkeep of different parts of the village. In earlier days there were probably many more wooded areas and Bradley Woods may have been part of the much larger Sherwood Forest of those legendary days of Robin Hood. Records state that there was a skirmish between Royalist and the Parliamentarians at the foot of nearby Kirklees Woods in 1643.

The name of Bradley actually appears in the *Domesday Book* in 1086, but it is found under the name *Bradelia*, possibly coming from the term 'Broad Lea', meaning a wide meadow. There were wide meadows here as well in the early days, along with the wooded areas. A record in the *Domesday Book* states: 'Godwin and Deflin held three carucates of land to be taxed and two ploughs might be employed there. Now Chetel holds it of Ilbert but it is waste. TRE it was valued at or paid £3. Wood pasture one mile and a half long and one broad.' A carucate was equal to 120 acres. Ilbert was Ilbert de Lacy, the Lord of Pontefract, and he was also a great supporter of William the Conqueror. TRE is an abbreviation for *Tempore regis Edwardi*, in the time of King Edward (the Confessor). So the name of Bradley is over 900 years old.

The centre of the village has changed a number of times over the centuries due to various industries, coming starting up and sadly closing down. It was thought that there could have been a track winding its way up from Cooper Bridge up to the Monks' Granary, which was possibly on the site of the present Bradley Grange.

The original small hamlet of around twelve families has grown to a very large estate. The old Bradley changed its size in the 1950s when the Corporation Estate was built. With this new estate came many other services that must go with so many new dwelling houses – a Roman Catholic church, more shops, the Little John public house, Hartley Manor Residential Home for the aged, a children's home, and of course the school. The building of this estate swallowed up many acres of farmland, including the land of Cinderfield Farm which was run for many years by the Stead family.

The Roll of the Subsidy granted in 1523 to Henry VIII brings us close to the time when the Huddersfield estates were acquired in great quantities by the Ramsden family. The subsidy was granted to enable the king to carry on the war with the French king, 'For the conservation of his honour, and for the revenging of the wrongs to his Highness and subjects.' This subsidy was not a poll or head count tax, but a levy on lands, goods and wages. The tax to be paid was one shilling in the pound of land value and sixpence in the pound for the value of goods. The mark was 13s 4d; and such an expression as 'five marklands' meant that lands assessed at five marks or £3 6s 8d.

From the records it indicated only two persons from Bradley were taxed. Arthur Pilkington (£40 of land; taxed at 40s), and John Cay (£40 worth of goods; taxed at 20 shillings.)

It has been said that if Rip Van Winkle had fallen asleep during Henry VIII's reign and then awakened during the early eighteenth century, the countryside around Bradley would have been exactly the same. It is thought that around 1547 Bradley Hall may have been the original site of the grange and may have been also a corn mill. The existing Old Corn Mill public house on the Brighouse Road is thought to be on the opposite side of the river to the original Bradley Hall. In the seventeenth and eighteenth centuries the centre of the village was not at Bradley Hall but the area where the two main roads form a junction at Oak Lane and Bradley Lane. Oak Lane was not far from where the Keldregate bus terminus is now sited.

The importance of the main routes from Bradley to the adjoining monastic properties necessitated the provision of the two bridges at Cooper Bridge and Colne Bridge to give greater and better access to Bradley Hall and the hamlet. Stoney Lane, which is adjacent to the existing Bradley Grange, was possibly built on the site of the original Fountains Abbey grange, giving a 'causey' for many

an eighteenth-century packhorse. Maps indicate that it was not called 'Stoney Lane', but Steeplands. The word 'causey' comes from 'causeway'. Causeys were usually raised up on a bank and were used as a footpath at the side of a sunken lane. The horse and cart traffic would cause the lanes to be grooved and sunken. They would be the routes taken by the local farmers and travellers. Obviously these sunken lanes were far better for travelling on during the fine weather. The causeys would provide a good track for the pedestrians and even packhorses in all kinds of weather.

These routes of unaltered track can still be followed in some places today in our local area. One can be picked up at Shepherds Thorn Lane and followed from the Bradley Wood Scouts campsite on Bradford Road where it crosses over the motorway and into Brighouse. There is now a modern footbridge that crosses over the motorway. This track crosses over Bradley Road and continues down into Wiggan Lane at Sheepridge. It has a sunken path with a slightly raised causey with some stretches having paving stones. But, sadly, in some places nature takes over and some of the routes become overgrown with shrubs and weeds.

There is a track that runs between Wiggan Lane and Bradley Road that is called Old Lane. It is uncertain where it acquired the name. It is possible that it took its name from a house that was called 'Old House', as many roads did in those early days, as in the name of Bradley Gate which took its name from Bradley Gate House. The 1854 Ordnance Survey map shows five buildings near to Bradley Gate House; two were on one side of Old Lane and three on the opposite side. They have long been destroyed and the only sign of their existence is the nettles that can be seen there during the summer months. Nettles grow where people and animals have left their waste such as ash pits, stables, etc. When people and animals vacate their habitat the phosphate remains from the waste last for many more years and many weeds will take advantage of this and quite often grow in abundance. Old Lane continues to rise through the fields and up to Lower Fell Greave Wood. There is the story of girl who fell in love with a young man who lived in Toothill. The girl's father did not approve of this courtship and forbade his daughter to see this man. The man sent a letter to his girlfriend and tied it to his dog. Sadly the girl's father discovered the dog with its mission and he cut off its head with one swing of his sword. The animal ran around headless around Fell Greave Wood for some time. Upset by this the young man left the area and his sweetheart longed for him to return and she died of a broken heart. For many a year after these supposed events the ghost of a young lady was seen walking through her home area of Newhouse. The dog's ghost is supposed to terrify anyone who is brave enough to enter the Fell Greave Wood during a moonlight night.

From very early days the wooded land that surrounded Bradley played a very important part of the everyday life and economy of the village. Much of the wood was used for the provision of fuel, as charcoal was the main requirement of fuel for the forges belonging to the monastic ironworks. Even in those days they still considered conservation, as the trees that were to be chopped down were to be at least eighteen years in growth.

The sale of Bradley Manor and the Freehold Estate of Bradley was held at the Public Sale Room in Southampton Buildings, Chancery Lane, London, on Tuesday 24 May 1830 starting at 12 noon. These words were recorded on the introduction page to the sale guide booklet: 'The title to the Bradley estate comprises indentures of the lease and release dated 1 and 2 February 1705. The said estate was conveyed to Sir Lyon Pilkington, in fee, and has ever since been the possession of the family. This sale comprised the Manor or Lordship of Bradley, with the Capital and other Messuages, cottages, mills, extensive woods, plantations, coal mines, stone quarries and about 400 acres of woodland, 800 acres of valuable meadow, pasture and arable land, divided into convenient farms, and in the occupation of a very respectable tenantry, at low rents. This estate lies entirely within a Ring Fence, abounds in coal of an excellent quality, and is bordered on two sides by navigational canals, and is surrounded by woods forming part of the estate.' The whole estate was exempt from the payment of the Great Tythes, but was subject to Land Tax of £31 9s 9d and Small Tythes of £10.

A complaint was received on 10 August 1868 from the Canal Company regarding a nuisance caused by Mr John Dransfield's family throwing their dirty water over the wall and into the company's yard. An anonymous letter was received at that same meeting complaining of the nuisance caused by Mr Isaac Cliffe's pigs and sty. Mr John Brierley, Chairman, had received information of a nuisance in the Quarry

Plantation, being one dead horse that had only been partially buried. Mr Abnor Hill, woodman, was given notice to bury the same 4ft down and within 24 hours. These few items indicate just some of the work considered by the Bradley Local Board.

During the early nineteenth century, the roads were becoming quite busy around Huddersfield, so it was decided to install toll houses on the main thoroughfares and it is believed that there were three sited around Bradley. One was situated at the top of Church Lane close to where the Woodman Inn now stands. It collected money from the traffic using the Leeds Road. A second toll house was located at the top of Bradley Lane and collected tolls there in 1822. In 1759 Bradley Lane was upgraded to be part of the Dewsbury and Elland turnpike road, which in turn formed the main part of the trade route from Wakefield across to Lancashire. A bar house was situated on Bradley Road just below the junction of Shepherds Thorn Lane and Bradley Road, which managed somehow to survive until sometime in the 1940s. It had been situated there to catch some of the travellers on that road who would try hard not to pay the toll by slipping down the Old Road. Bradley therefore became a very important crossroads for traffic using the Leeds-Manchester and Dewsbury-Elland roads.

In 1822 tolls were levied on all horses, mules, asses and other beasts or cattle that were towing any wagon, wain, caravan, cart or van, depending on the sizes of the fellies. Fellies were the width of the wheels at the bottom or sole. All horses, asses, mules or other beasts or cattle either loaded with cargo or without and not towing anything were charged at the rate of 1d. For every twenty oxen, cows or neat cattle the cost was 10d. For every twenty of calves, pigs, sheep or lambs the levy was 5d. But the cost came higher to those vehicles that were self-propelled. For every carriage that moved or was propelled by steam or machinery, or by any other power that was not provided by an animal, the charge was 10s 6d.

B. Farren

The Eland Feud: A Medieval Huddersfield Murder

Introduction
In the West Riding in the fourteenth century a series of murders occurred which have become known as the Eland Feud. The events, for the most part, took place in the districts around Huddersfield, such as Lockwood, Quarmby, Crosland Moor, Holmfirth, Skelmanthorpe, Brighouse and Almondbury. The story of the Feud has since remained part of Huddersfield's history and the men at its centre have become part of a local legend, with the concepts of good and evil, revenge and justice at its core.[1] But rarely does legend follow the truth.

A historical examination of the Eland Feud in some ways resembles the criminal investigation of a murder. It has its own set of witnesses, motives and list of suspects. Such an investigation may determine whether the Feud was the *crime passionnel* often quoted or a cold-blooded murder carried out by ruthless perpetrators, for no more noble a reason than self-preservation.

The Witnesses

A short discussion should be made regarding the credibility of our sources. There is no one all-inclusive fourteenth-century source and, like witnesses of a crime, when compared, they often demonstrate discrepancies in their statements. The official documents provide invaluable information but they remain impassive.[2] The source with the most passion is a sixteenth-century ballad but it is also the one with the most problems.[3] Historians have often used this as the main reference for the facts, yet the date and the author's alternative agenda make it far less reliable than a contemporary source.[4] As we will see, there are numerous problems with the witnesses' statements; nevertheless it would be dangerous to underestimate any of them. Each statement is invaluable and is our insight into the past.

The Crime

The murders of Sir John Eland and his son, also named John, have formed the basis of the Eland Feud; however, various other elements have been added as the story has been told and retold. Discovering the real crime is not necessarily an easy task. But as with any criminal investigation we must ascertain the facts of the crime in order to discover the perpetrator.

So let us begin with what we do know. Sir John Eland was murdered on 29 October 1350 somewhere in the vicinity of Brighouse, although it is unlikely that he was returning from the Tourn, the twice-yearly manorial court, as traditionally stated in the Ballad.[5] An indictment issued on 9 April 1351, obviously unseen or ignored by the author

of the Ballad, confirms his death.[6] As Appendix 1 of this study shows, the death of his son John was also officially documented, although this time the specific date is less easy to ascertain. The Ballad states that it was on the Palm Sunday following his father's death,[7] and later historians have been inclined to agree.[8] We do know that the younger John Eland was dead by 6 July 1351 when a commission was established appointing the local Justices of the Peace to 'take the said felons and such others as the justices shall furnish names of and bring them to the gaol of York',[9] but there are no contemporary documents confirming either the exact date or location.

Evidence for the murder of the other alleged victims is even more ambiguous. These supposedly included an unknown kinsman of Sir John Eland, Sir Robert Beaumont, his brother William, Hugh of Quarmby, Lockwood of Lockwood, Sir John's grandson and various servants and retainers.[10] The latter of these are known to have been caught up in the trouble, but exactly who they were and how many can not be ascertained.[11] But it is the deaths of the other men which are of the most interest, for it is these which, according to tradition, began the feud. Further research has found that while Sir Robert Beaumont died in 1330, John of Quarmby was still alive until 1336.[12] The only crimes therefore which constitute the Eland Feud are the murders of Sir John and his son. This has enormous consequences for our consideration of the motive.

The Motive

There is an adage in most detective fiction that if you can find the motive for a murder you can find the perpetrator. It is a theory which holds some weight and one which, to a certain degree, can be applied to the Eland Feud. Over the centuries several theories have been proposed but many of these have been based on historical hearsay rather than solid evidence.

The most obvious of these is the theory that Eland and his son were killed as part of the larger, more significant, feud between the Earls of Warenne and Lancaster. This was first proposed in 1629 and claimed that the Earls' quarrel over Lancaster's wife extended down into the localities.[13] But the dates of the two events are contradictory; Lancaster's quarrel with Warenne took place in 1317 and, indeed, Lancaster was dead by 1322, whilst the Eland Feud occurred in 1350-

1351. The possibility that conflicting affinities erupted into open violence in the West Riding so long after the initial events is highly unlikely. Over enthusiasm by historians to connect local and national politics, and the involvement of Thomas Lascy, the family name of the Earls of Lancaster, caused the Eland Feud to be mistakenly linked to a larger national crisis. We should eliminate this theory as a motive.

Yet the idea of a feud sparked by murder and revenge between local gentry families has remained prominent, largely due to the evidence provided by the Ballad.[14] But the substantial discrepancies in its testimony indicate a problem. Recorded instances of Lockwood and Quarmby being in Yorkshire before their supposed return in 1350 plus Adam

Linthwaite in the Colne Valley, West Yorkshire.

Beaumont's age, between twenty-nine and thirty-two, suggests that they did not return at the earliest opportunity to seek their revenge.[15] But, why would they return to seek revenge when, as we have seen, their fathers were not murdered in the first place?

The contemporary sources, meanwhile, offer no evidence of conflict between the families before 1350. There are no pleas of debt, theft or trespass or any other incidents of criminal activity by one against the other appearing in the local court records.[16] The problems with the Ballad's explanation and the lack of evidence of conflict in other sources would suggest that there may be a further motive for the crime. A more conceivable explanation is that the attack on Sir John Eland was due to the threat he posed to the liberty of some of West Yorkshire's criminal fraternity.[17]

There are two prominent pieces of evidence which suggest that the motives for the Eland murders were Sir John's pursuit of the local criminals and his son's pursuit of justice. The first is the indictment for the murder of Sir John which clearly states that he was killed because his killers were 'indicted before the said Sir John and his colleagues of various felonies and trespasses, and process by capias and exigent was issuing against them…'.[18] Furthermore, Sir John was not their only intended victim, and another justice, William Mirfield, was lucky to escape a similar attack.[19]

The second piece of evidence is equally clear. The order for a commission, detailed in Appendix 1, states that Sir John's son was killed '…because he was suing before the king to punish them for his father's death'. In both cases it would seem that the actual motive for the killings was not revenge but self-preservation. Sir John was the unfortunate victim of an attack on the man in office rather than on him personally and in drawing up his will on 8 September 1350 indicates that he was aware of the danger.[20]

The Suspects

This motive could lead to thousands of possible suspects. Anyone that Sir John Eland had come into contact with, especially if accompanied by William Mirfield, could have a motive. But we have a witness who makes it quite clear who contemporaries believed to be responsible. Several entries in the *Calendar of Patent Rolls* and the indictment for the murder of Sir John specifically name Adam Beaumont, William Lockwood and William Quarmby as well as 'very many other felons'.[21]

Adam Beaumont's role in the murders is the most complex. He is depicted in the Ballad as the primary conspirator in the attack, and the official records always specifically name him. The Beaumont family certainly had a colourful past, but it is Adam's elder brother, Sir John Beaumont, who would seem to have the greater motive. He was involved in various criminal activities including a physical assault and theft in 1340, which probably brought him into contact with Sir John who was then the Sheriff, and a murder in 1341.[22] Adam is less prolifically mentioned in the records than John. He appears only once in the *Records of the King's Bench*, in 1344, and even then there is some room for doubt, as the name recorded is Adam Paumont.[23]

Without the unambiguous statement in

the *Calendar of Patent Rolls* it would be John who would be the primary suspect. Perhaps the officials dealing with the case named the wrong brother, but he is named so often that it is unlikely that the error would have been made so many times. It could also have been possible that Adam was acting on behalf of John. But until the murders, Adam may simply have been one of a gang rather than a prolific criminal mind, and somehow found himself thrust, deservedly or otherwise, to the fore by 1350. Certainly by 6 July 1351 Beaumont was a key member of a gang that was responsible not only for the Eland murders but also for attacks on several other justices.[24] It is impossible to dismiss him from the list of suspects with such clear statements at our disposal.

It was Lockwood and Quarmby who had the greatest motive. In March 1350 they were in serious trouble with the law and Sir John was amongst a list of men, including William Mirfield, ordered to bring the men to trial 'on account of felonies and trespasses in the West Riding Co. York'.[25] Five months later, Sir John Eland was dead, and Lockwood and Quarmby were known to be at large, despite the order to detain them.[26] Like Adam Beaumont, Lockwood and Quarmby are usually specifically named in the orders and with motive, opportunity and a 'witness account' these two men seem the likeliest suspects.

Of course they did not act alone. The ambushes on the Elands were carried out by a host of armed men, but none, other than Thomas Lascy, are named. However, several Huddersfield men were later identified as co-conspirators. Although none were convicted Robert del Bothe,

Richard del Bothe, Mathew de Hepworth, Thomas Lister of Almondbury, Ralph de Skelmanthorpe, Edmund de Flocton and John de Shelley were all arrested for being involved with at least one of the main protagonists.[27] There is little evidence of any of them being in serious trouble with the manorial court before this date. Robert del Bothe of Holmfirth appears continuously throughout the period 1348-1352, but his usual crime is a plea of debt or a fine for illegal brewing, contempt of court or not controlling his pigs.[28] He did, however, have an on-going dispute with Sir William de Skarghill, one of the justices later involved in the investigation of Sir John's murder, and it is possible that he met Ralph Skelmanthorpe when both were jurors at the Tourn on 27 November 1348.[29] But other than this there is little evidence to connect them with each other or with Beaumont, Lockwood and Quarmby.

Conclusion

The case against Beaumont, Quarmby and Lockwood seems almost conclusive. They are named by most witnesses and all had the opportunity. Although legend has engendered the idea that the gang sort revenge against an evil sheriff for the unjust deaths of their fathers, additional evidence would suggest otherwise. The fact that the elder generations did not die as suggested by the Ballad, and that Beaumont, Quarmby and Lockwood were known to be prolific criminals in the area, throws serious doubt on their defence of a *crime passionnel*. But ultimately it is the testimony of the official documents, both clearly naming the three main suspects, which indicates that the motive was cold-blooded self-preservation. As such, we must conclude that the defendants are guilty as charged.

Bibliography

Published primary sources

Calendar of Patent Rolls 1348-1350 Vol. 8, Nendeln/Liechtenstein, 1971.

Calendar of Patent Rolls 1350-1354 Vol. 9, Nendeln/Liechtenstein, 1971.

Calendar of Patent Rolls 1354-1358 Vol. 10, Nendeln/Liechtenstein, 1971.

Habberjam, M., O'Regan, M. and Hale, B., eds The Court Rolls of the Manor of Wakefield October 1350 to September 1352, Yorkshire Archaeological Society, 1987.

Jewell, H.M., ed. The Court Rolls of the Manor of Wakefield from September 1348 to September 1350, Yorkshire Archaeological Society, 1981.

Paley Baildon, W., ed. 'The Elland Feud', The Yorkshire Archaeological Journal 11 (1891), pp. 128-130.

Secondary Sources

Dyson, T. The History of Huddersfield and District, 2nd ed. Huddersfield, 1951.

Kaye, J.M. 'The Eland Murders 1350-1: A Study of the Legend of the Eland Feud', The Yorkshire Archaeological Journal 51 (1979), pp. 61-79.

Watson, J. The History and Antiquities of the Parish of Halifax in Yorkshire, London, 1775.

'Dodworth's Note of the Feud between Eland and Beaumont MS cxlv f107', The Yorkshire Archaeological Journal 2 (1873), pp. 124-127.

Appendix 1

From Calendar of Patent Rolls 1350-1354, p. 156; 6 July 1351

Commission to William de Plumpton, Brian de Thornhill, William de Skarghill, the elder, Nicholas de Wortelay, Henry de Sothill, John de Calverlay, Thomas Flemmyng, Robert de Staynton, Adam de Hopton, John Tours, Aymer Burdet, William de Mirfield, John de Sheffield, William de Lewenthorp, William de Beston and Thomas de Fenton reciting that Adam Beaumund, William de Lokwode and very many other felons indicted of the death of John de Eland, one of the king's justices appointed to hear and determine trespasses in the West Riding, co. York, gathering to themselves a very great number of felons and evildoers have killed John son of the said John because he was suing before the king to punish them for his father's death, and many others of the household and friendship of the said John de Eland, and have committed various assaults on the king's justices appointed to hear and determine such homicides, felonies, trespasses and misdeeds, and killed some of their men and servants, and now strive to the utmost of their power to hinder those who indict them, the justices, the sheriff and other ministers of the king from executing his mandates and their offices, openly threatening them, and so to hinder if they can the king from ruling and doing justice to his people; and appointing them to take the said felons and such others as the justices shall furnish names of and bring them to the gaol of York. Wherefore the king commands them on pain of life and limbs and all that they can forfeit to be diligent in the execution of the premises.

Appendix 2

From Calendar of Patent Rolls 1348-1350, p. 530; 24 March 1350

Appointment of William Basset, John de Eland, Nicolas de Wortele and William de Notton to deliver the gaol of York Castle of William de Horneby son of William de Querneby and William son of Thomas de Lokwod, detained there on account of felonies and trespasses in the West Riding, co. York, whereof they are indicted before the same William Basset, John and Nicolas, and Robert de Nevill of Horneby, Thomas de Fencotes, Brian de Thornhill, Thomas de Seton, Roger de Blaykeston, William de Fyncheden, William de Mirfield and John de Northland, appointed as keepers of the peace and justices to hear and determine divers felonies and trespasses in that Riding; as the king is informed that the said William and William purpose to procure their deliverance fraudulently by suborned or procured jurors, by mainprise, or by some other means.

For end notes please see p. 85.

For end notes please see p. 85.

Samantha Yalden

Slaithwaite: An Old Railway Line

Unless facts are recorded and written down we depend upon the memories of people who lived at the time to tell us about the state of things in the past. In this instance I depend on the experiences and memories of my father and grandfather.

The railway line through the Colne Valley was opened in 1849 so the old stone-built Slaithwaite station must have been built at about that time. It had four tracks running through it and there were also sidings on the south side which enabled coal-trucks to go to the coal chutes to be emptied of their contents. The station was demolished in 1968 together with the coal chutes, following the Beeching Report. The site of the old chutes can still be seen and identified today, although much overgrown by vegetation.

A much less well-known fact is that on the north side of Slaithwaite station was a siding which went westwards towards the viaduct and then went across Bank Gate to the Bank Gate Mills. In those days the mills were doing a brisk trade in shoddy and had their own wagons for conveying the materials. There is no sign of this railway line today and indeed the landscape has so changed from excavation and the building of walls that there would now be no access to the station from Bank Gate. However, if one stands in Bank Gate it can be seen that the mills and the viaduct are on the same level.

My father knew the old coal chutes well, as his work as a youth was to check in the coal-trucks and record the load of coal each carried and discharged. My father told me about the railway track across Bank Gate and it may have been there when he was a boy. He was born in 1884. It was certainly there in my grandfather's time and he lived from 1852 to 1916.

There is no record of the line on a large-scale map of 1890 so it seems likely that this branch-line had a short existence after that date. The prosperity of the mills declined, so presumably there was no further need for the line. I cannot give the dates when the line was constructed or removed but there may be some record in the local newspapers of that period.

Philip Dransfield

The view of Bank Gate, Slaithwaite, from the railway viaduct, looking north. The railway track crossed the road at the level of the viaduct.

Dangers and Delights of the Holmfirth Railway

The weather on the morning of 1 July 1850 was that of a typical English summer, with the rain coming down in buckets for most of the day. In spite of this, the church bells rang out, calling thousands of people to witness a marvellous event – the opening of the Holmfirth branch of the Lancashire and Yorkshire Railway.

Trains had been used since 1825 to carry coal and other goods, but the first passenger-carrying trains, run by the Liverpool and Manchester Railway, were not in service until 1830. With the arrival of passenger trains, the psychology of travel was transformed – for the first time,

it was possible to get from A to B at speeds faster than a horse. The effects of the railways on the movement of goods and on the minds of the people cannot be underestimated – 'railway mania' is a perfect description!

Although Huddersfield was only connected to the Manchester railway in 1849, the huge crowds which turned out to see the opening of the Holmfirth branch show that people were hugely fascinated by this new method of transport. George Sykes, an inhabitant of Holmfirth, noted that even in the early years of the twentieth century, 'on special occasions and Sundays, it was quite the thing to go to the railway station to watch the people come off the train.' Train journeys were a great adventure, although most people in the Holme Valley could not afford the fares at first. Cloth manufacturers and other tradesmen took advantage of the speed of the railway to sell their wares faster and further afield, leading to greater prosperity for the valley as a whole.

The Holmfirth branch, although much used and loved, had its share of problems and predicaments. Within a month of the line opening, the railway company received complaints from passengers who had turned up at Holmfirth station to find that their train had already left. The cause of the problem? The station clock, which ran on standardized 'railway time', was fifteen minutes ahead of the clock on the parish church, which ran on 'local time'! This discrepancy may have been the inspiration for a story in the *Holmfirth*

Almanack of 1929, when a planned trip to Blackpool begins badly and gets worse. The storyteller relates: 'As wi passed church clock it wor just leaving foive an' twenty minutes to six, soa wi thowt wi'd plenty o' time, an' wi took it varry steady, but just as wi walked on to' th platform train wor starting off, an' as wi wor nother directors not shareholders, pooarter wodn't stop it for us to get in.'

By 1896, twenty passenger trains and six goods trains were leaving Holmfirth station each day. Before the line opened, people would grumble about having to walk all the way to Huddersfield. After the Holmfirth branch came into existence, laziness hit an all-time high when people began to grumble about having to walk to the station! Fashions of the time also caused problems – the

Mytholmbridge viaducts near Holmfirth.

railway company received complaints from ladies whose tight skirts made it difficult for them to climb into the carriages! In a wonderful example of customer services, the directors had the platform of Holmfirth station raised to eliminate the difficulty.

More seriously, a potential disaster was averted in August 1852 by the quick thinking if Thomas Normington, the guard of an excursion train returning to Holmfirth from Hull. The train was twenty-five carriages long, and packed full of people, meaning that it was too heavy for the engine to pull up the slight gradient between Thongsbridge and Holmfirth. This was quite a common occurrence, solved by detaching half of the carriages and taking half of the train to the station. The engine would then return to pick up the abandoned passengers and take them home. On this particular night, however, another engine came racing up the line towards the stranded carriages. Normington seized a red lamp and tore up the track. Thankfully, he managed to stop the engine just in time – just twelve inches short of the carriages full of holidaymakers!

Far more horrific was the macabre trainload which arrived in the aftermath of the devastating Holmfirth Flood of 5 February 1852. Eighty-one people in the Holme Valley were killed on that terrible night as the banks of Bilberry Reservoir burst and 86 million gallons of water cascaded down onto the unsuspecting villages. Damage at the time was estimated at over £250,000 and 7,038 people were put out of work. As the survivors attempted to clear the mess of rubble, water, machinery, mud and corpses, and to identify the bodies which had been laid out in the public houses, the Holmfirth train brought 300 sightseers from Manchester who had come on a specially-arranged excursion to view the damage. Needless to say, they did not receive a very warm welcome.

Thirteen years later, in 1865, another structure collapsed which could have caused a similar loss of life; by a miraculous stroke of luck, not one person was hurt. When the Holmfirth line was constructed, a viaduct was needed to span the valley to Thongsbridge station. To save on costs, the Mytholmbridge viaduct was made from wood rather than stone, despite the fact that the wooden Denby Dale viaduct had fallen down in a great storm on 17 January 1847. Just before this collapse, a junior porter on the Denby Dale line, whose job it was to fill the fire buckets on the viaduct, said that he could only half-fill them – whenever a train passed over it, the viaduct vibrated so much that most of the water spilled out! Contemporary photographs of wooden railway viaducts show alarmingly rickety-looking structures, and passengers often refused to cross them. Fear of the viaducts was so widespread that the Lancashire and Yorkshire Railway Company went as far as commissioning a survey from the great Robert Stephenson on the Denby Dale and the Mytholmbridge viaducts. His report concluded, 'you may rest assured that both structures are perfectly safe.' Not everyone was convinced by this, and in 1864, the directors were concerned enough to order the construction of a stone viaduct. Building work began, but cracks began to appear in the stones. On 3 December 1865, the viaduct collapsed entirely, taking the old wooden viaduct with it. By a piece of fantastic good fortune, the new structure fell early on a Sunday morning, so none of the workmen were on it at the time. Even more luckily, the 7 a.m. train from Huddersfield was stopped at Brockholes just before the viaduct fell; an hour later and the collapse would have caused a horrific disaster. Part of the branch line remained closed for two years while a new contractor rebuilt the viaduct, and Holmfirth passengers had to use horse-drawn omnibuses to take them to Honley, from where they could catch their trains.

Not all of the stories connected with the Holmfirth branch are filled with doom and disaster. Railway mania meant that people could go to places which would once have been too far away to consider visiting. Mass tourism was born, and the people of the Holme Valley were not slow to take advantage of their new freedom. On Honley Feast in 1851, around 1,190 passengers travelled from Holmfirth to Huddersfield. Honley also became a hot tourist spot around forty years later with the opening of the Hope Bank Pleasure Gardens. Containing two lakes, thirty rowing boats, a steamer, a switchback and additional extras such as dancing and roller-skating, Hope Bank was the Alton Towers of its day – in fact, publicity from the early 1900s advertises it as the 'New Blackpool'. People flocked from miles around to experience its charms.

In 1852, a cheap train excursion to Penistone was organized one Sunday evening which attracted 3,000 people from Holmfirth. Sadly, the Penistone infrastructure could not cope with the sheer numbers of tourists and the pubs ran dry! This curious tale shows how the powerful combination of the Holmfirth branch line and the lure of foreign beer even managed to overturn Sunday religious observances.

The growing fame of the Denby Dale Pie drew crowds of tourists from the Holme Valley whenever it was cooked, and special events in Huddersfield also attracted people from neighbouring districts. For example, in 1884 Greenhead Park opened, complete with bandstand, lake, flowerbeds, tennis courts, playground, Italian gardens and bowling greens, and many people came by train to admire the new leisure grounds.

Excursions to the seaside became increasingly popular, with trains of around 500 to 600 of the Holmfirth populace travelling to Blackpool, Scarborough and Bridlington. In 1851, some intrepid explorers used the train to travel all the way to London, drawn by the lure of the Great Exhibition. Records do not show how many people from this area attended the Exhibition as tourists, but exhibitors' lists show the presence of Holmfirth manufacturers who no doubt used the improved transport network to show off their goods in the city.

Closer to home, people in 1917 were delighted by a new service which was born in Holmfirth. George Willie Castle and Joseph Bower originally set up a system of small vans to collect passengers from the Honley tram. When they saw how popular it was, they extended their service and began picking up passengers from the last train at Holmfirth station. Castle was a baker, and he fitted seats to his bakery van to create a new 'shuttle service'. Delighted Holmfirth residents christened it the 'Bun Van', and stories and anecdotes collected from elderly people in the town show that the van is still fondly remembered. Castle and Bower's success inspired two other companies to compete for custom – 'HMS', run by Wilson Haigh, and the 'Yellow Peril', a double decker run by the Baddeley Brothers, although neither seem to have won such a firm place in Holmfirth hearts as the old bread delivery van.

The Holmfirth branch continued to link the Holme Valley with the wider world, but the general decline of the railways after the First World War spelled disaster for the line. The railway system was nationalized in 1947, by which time it had become run down and was in need of structural repairs and modernization. The last passenger train from Holmfirth ran in 1959, and Richard Beeching, who became chairman of the British Railways Board in 1963, struck the final blow. His scheme of 'rationalization' sounded the death knell for the British railway system, drastically cutting back on train services and closing down branch lines. In 1965, the Beeching cuts reached the Holmfirth branch; the last goods service was terminated and the line closed down. Now, the land around the two former stations of Thongsbridge and Holmfirth is unrecognizable. Modern housing developments cover the ground where booking office, platform, sidings, tracks and turntables used to stand. The shutting down of our branch line was and is a great loss to Holmfirth. One local remembers going to Blackpool from Holmfirth station, commenting, 'It used to be a thriving place, everybody used to go on holiday from there.' Our trains will never return, but the past loss of the Holmfirth branch is a good reminder for

the present – we should not take our public services for granted, but should treasure them and fight for them, both for ourselves and for our children.

Bibliography

Bullock, P. & I., *The Archive Photographs Series: Holme Valley* (1995).

Cannon, J. (ed.), *The Oxford Companion to British History* (1997).

Crystal, David (ed.), *The Cambridge Paperback Encyclopedia* (1999).

Field, K., & Stephenson, B., *Pennine Steam* (1977).

'A Day's Yat', *Holmfirth Almanack*, 1929, p. 49.

The Holmfirth Flood (1910)

Kemp, W., *Holmfirth by Lamplight* (1987).

Lane, B.C., *The Holmfirth Branch* (1984)

Scott, B. (ed.), *Where the Pratty Flowers Grow: voices from Holmfirth* (1988).

Williams, E., *Holmfirth from forest to township* (1975).

Fran Parnell

Moonraking in Slaithwaite

Light up your lantern, light up your light;
Remember your friends on this cold frosty night.
Light up your lantern, light up your light
We're out Moonraking, our spirits are bright.

The moon she has fallen out of the sky,
She lies in canal with a tear in her eye.
Bring out your rake, hook her out, keep her dry;
Take her round Slawit' and hold her up high.

Moonraking Woodcut by Adam Strickson.

At night in the Colne Valley, the street lamps and the houses look like glow worms, resting on the valley hillside, clusters of warm twinkling light. They lie still, but for one night every year when many beautiful lanterns join them, which, carried by their makers, wind their way down to the Huddersfield Narrow Canal for the Slaithwaite Moonraking. Everyone gathers by an old stone bridge, songs are sung, a brass band plays and a large willow and paper lantern moon is pulled along the canal on a raft. Its reflection on the water disperses as villagers with long rakes attempt to pull it out onto the bank. Comic characters dressed as gnomes with wispy beards succeed in landing the moon, by ingenious use of a hand-made wooden crane. They hook it out through a loop in its nose. It is lifted onto a bamboo stretcher and carried round the village accompanied by a host of villagers of all ages carrying their candle-lit lantern creations. Musicians, jugglers, costumed characters and fire-eaters add to the warmth and excitement of this annual winter carnival. The procession meanders up Bankgate, a steep hill, to the streets of Hilltop. People come out of their houses or wave from windows as it passes by. The destination is the Colne Valley Leisure Centre, where when the parade arrives, hundreds of participants blow out their lanterns and enter the sports hall for a festive family knees-up and much-needed refreshment.

This event has become a celebration of living in the Colne Valley and has been re-enacted in Slaithwaite during February

The Lantern Moon.

story was elaborated upon by the arrival of a Giant Moon Moth. This fantastical insect flew in attracted by the light of the moon and the villager's lanterns. In this version of the story the moon moth rescues the moon from the canal and takes it back up into the sky. This links with an oriental legend of a Japanese Moon Moth that flies to the moon and back. There is a similar moth in the adventure stories of Doctor Doolittle written by Hugh Lofting.

The Colne Valley has a number of such legends that form the basis of a wide variety of colourful seasonal festivities through out the calendar of the year. The cycle begins with Imbolc, a fire festival that marks the end of the winter solstice. Slaithwaite Moonraking follows on in February followed by Cuckoo Day in Marsden in the spring. The Golcar Lilies celebrate their own story with a gala in the summer and Linthwaite's tale of The Leadboilers has recently been revived and is re-enacted as part of a folk festival based at the Sair Inn during the autumn.

The main focus of the week-long Moonraking Festival is the lantern-making workshops. These are held at Slaithwaite Community Centre, an old school, now well used by local community groups. The workshops are run by local artists and volunteers who have learnt over the years to make stunning sculptural lanterns. Help is always on hand for beginners and those who have been before inspire and assist also. The lantern framework is constructed from stripped willow sticks, joined together by masking tape to make large three-dimensional structures. Candles are fixed inside with wire and have a tin lid to catch the hot wax. The surface of the

for the past eighteen years. The Moonraking stories are however centuries old and different versions of the story have inspired the current revival. One of the original stories is that there were local smugglers who used to hide their bounty under the canal bridge when it arrived by canal boat from the sea. One night when the moon was full, the smugglers were caught by the militia trying to remove a barrel from under the bridge with a rake. The story goes that they escaped arrest by telling their captors that they were just out 'Moonraking', the reflection of the full moon being clearly seen in the water!

At the much more recent turn of the century 'Millennium Moonraking', the lantern is then covered with wet-strength tissue paper and watered down PVA glue. When the paper dries out it clings to the lantern shell and makes a tight waterproof skin. A paper door is cut in the side of it to allow a taper to reach the candle for lighting on the night. A wire loop is threaded into the top of the structure so that it can be carried on a bamboo with a wire hook. The shapes of the lanterns are linked by a different theme each year. In the early years one very successful idea was that people made lanterns shaped like their houses, so when all of them were lit and carried in procession Slaithwaite looked like a flying model village! More recent themes have been space, river creatures, fruit and vegetables and in one particularly icy winter a 'Polar Moonraking' was held with lanterns shaped like penguins, seals and icebergs! The lantern making workshops run for a week with delicious cakes and refreshments, made by the local branch of the Women's Institute. The Saturday evening procession and re-enactment of the story is the climax to the creative activity and whatever the weather the Slaithwaite Moonraking has always taken place.

Fact and fiction are mixed up in many local stories and images from today are added to enrich the stories of the past. In recent years Moonraking has seen lanterns depicting eco-warriors, submarines and even the Millennium Dome! Symbols from the present time find their place amidst a simple folk tale from the past about the moon, a rake, a barrel and a bridge! The event itself is almost tribal: a valley community celebrating its own local history with its own hand-made creativity. The procession, following a well-worn route around the village, parades joyfully with the glow of rosy faces caught by the light of their jostling lanterns. There is even a moment called 'the community scream' where everyone huddles together and whoops under an echoey railway bridge. This once a year event offers a welcome to those new and a reunion for friends of old, the candlelight from the lanterns sustaining warmth and community connectivity in the heart of the Colne Valley.

Andy Burton

Starkey's Mill, 1819-1907

In 1819, on a narrow strip of farmland at Longroyd Bridge, bounded by the curve of the canal on the north and the river Colne on the south, Starkey, Buckley & Co. began to raise what became, for many years, the largest woollen factory in Huddersfield. It is one of the ironies of Huddersfield's history that, only yards away, stood the cropping shop of John Wood where, seven years earlier, the Luddites had planned their campaign to halt the advance of machinery.

The main partners of the firm, Joseph, Thomas and John Starkey were woollen merchants who had previously undertaken some manufacturing in premises at Pedley's Mill, Paddock. They had accumulated enough wealth to buy a small mansion at Spring Dale, just across the river from where they established the mill. Expansion continued with the acquisition of three more plots of land at Longroyd Bridge in 1831. By the early

1830s the firm had become known simply as 'Starkey Brothers' and their premises, making plain woollen goods, was one of only a handful in the Huddersfield area deserving of the name factory, carrying out all the stages of manufacturing from the scribbling of wool to the dyeing and finishing of cloth. In 1833, the mills, powered by three 28hp steam engines, employed 521 people, 135 of them female and 73 of them under fourteen.[1]

The factory was one of the earliest to introduce power into woollen weaving and in 1835 it was reported that four power looms a week were being set up. A total of seventy were to be installed. Men were already being laid off, to be replaced, so it was later claimed, by cheaper female 'power loom tenters', paid an average of 7s 6d a week. Even this was reduced to 6s, resulting in a strike. It was estimated that a piece which a hand loom weaver had formerly produced for £3 now cost only 14s by power.[2]

The following year seventy-two pairs of power looms were insured for around £10 10s each, and the total machinery was valued at £18,654. The buildings were insured for about one third that of the machinery and comprised two five-storey mills for spinning, weaving and finishing; the four-storey Cross Factory (at right angles to the main east-west alignment of the buildings), for spinning; press shops, boiler house and stove; the Old Factory with three floors for scribbling and fulling; the East factory of five storeys for scribbling, spinning, finishing and the engine and boiler houses.[3]

The Starkey brothers were strongly opposed to the Ten Hour Act to limit child labour, being numbered among the 'Factory Mongers' by the radical *Voice of the West Riding*. Its editor, Joshua Hobson, cryptically alluded to the Starkey's lowly origins as 'back of the counter men… having some years ago tired of their call at Croppers Row and Commonside, next to the Poor House.' Thomas Starkey also supported the election campaign of the Whig candidate in 1833, further antagonizing working-class radicals. A notice was posted at the mill threatening to dismiss anyone whose absence from work coincided with a meeting of the Radical candidate, Captain Wood. Joseph Starkey was accused of 'exclusive dealing' (boycotting) by ordering his gardener not to buy seeds from a supplier who had voted for the pro-Ten Hour Bill Tory, Michael Sadler. The Starkey brothers were also actively opposed to trades unions, signing a resolution along with other manufacturers not to employ anyone 'who does not bring a good character in writing from his previous master' – that is a reference stating he was not a unionist. This probably accounts for the lack of evident union activity at the mill, apart from donations to strikers in Derby sent to Robert Owen's periodical the *Pioneer* by 'a few friends at Starkeys' Factory, Longroyd Bridge'. In 1839 the firm sacked seven workers, two of them with nineteen years' service, for their socialist opinions. One of these was the foreman of the dyeing department, George Brook, who had procured the site for the Socialists' Hall of Science. For him it proved a blessing in disguise, since he eventually established his own business at Larchfield Mills, Firth Street. One, possibly Brook himself, was unsuccessfully asked to return, since his replacement was damaging so much cloth. On the Saturday (13 August) of the 'Plug Riots' of 1842 strikers arrived at the mill gates. When Joseph Starkey, now a magistrate, read the Riot Act some of his men offered to help defend the mill, but the crowd forced their way in and 'plugged' the boilers, stopping the engines. An attempt to restart the mill on the following Monday was also thwarted.[4]

When, in 1844, it was reported that Thomas Starkey, 'the largest manufacturer in the neighbourhood', had implemented an eleven-hour day to help improve 'the morals and the habits' of the workers, reformers suspected this was really a ploy to undermine support for the Ten Hour Bill. George Brook Jnr claimed that the eleven-hour day had only been agreed after the Starkeys were satisfied that the equivalent of twelve hours of work could still be achieved. He listed this and other injustices – including the dismissal of his father, the displacement of men by women power loom weavers and of skilled wool-sorters by apprentices – on a poster attacking Joseph Starkey, the unsuccessful Conservative candidate in the 1853 election. To refute the accusations, which resulted in a libel charge against Brook, 282 foremen and workpeople signed a testimonial in support of Starkey, asserting that the eleven-hour day was introduced sincerely. Apparently there was not total contentment at the mill. In 1848 the giggers, who hand raised the cloth, suffered a wage reduction from 20s to 18s following the introduction of the Ten Hour Act. However a shilling was restored and they were given a sovereign back-pay. In 1860 female slubbers and layers-on resorted to a strike for an extra shilling to bring their wages up to that of other firms.[5]

The Starkeys combined patriarchal authority with paternalistic concern, assuming responsibility for the moral improvement and welfare of their workers. After Thomas Starkey's death from typhus in 1847, contracted, it was said, through helping a sick waif, his widow and brother John founded the imposing St Thomas's church as a memorial, just across the road from the mill. In 1849, during the cholera outbreak, the firm agreed with Dr Allatt of Paddock to pay workers' medical bills. Efforts were made to sterilize the mill by spreading chloride of lime. The workers 'spontaneously signed a memorial to the firm embodying their thanks in homely but heartfelt praise' for the care shown. Education was promoted by the financing of two schools. To encourage thrift, the workers and foremen set up a committee to form a savings bank in 1850. The mill also became a focus for recreational activities as loyalty was fostered by a works cricket team (which played, for example, against Victoria Mill, Lockwood in 1852) and treats and trips became a regular feature of mill life.[6]

In 1861 a tea was laid on for the burlers to encourage the speedy completion of an order and in June 1862 600 workers, plus 400 friends, went on a train excursion to Liverpool. As a treat the following day Lewis Starkey announced that, despite depression, there had been no short-time working and, to loud cheers, 'impressed upon the workpeople that so strong was the desire … to keep them in full work that they were prepared to sacrifice rather than close the mill'. The next year the 600 workers were also given an extra day's paid holiday.. The workforce showed its gratitude for the employer's benevolence by presenting a tea

Springdale Mills, from the west, lining the north bank of the river Colne.

service to one of the partners, Thomas Walker Brook, in 1874. At the ceremony tribute was paid to good relations in the firm and the fact that no short time had been worked in forty years. A foreman, Richard Moody, said he had been employed there for thirty-three years. This wasn't a record. The obituary of 'Old Ebenezer' Stanhope in 1891 referred to the thrity-five years he had worked for Starkeys. Isaac Suthers of Paddock, who died in 1895 aged seventy-nine, spent sixty-four years of his life at the mill! Some of the old employees received pensions from the firm but it was claimed others ended up in the workhouse.[7]

Even the great Huddersfield weavers' strike of 1883 had little adverse impact on industrial relations. Only about thirty of the weavers were in the Weavers' Association and there was no grievance with the firm because the disputed pay scales were not introduced. Nor were Starkey Bros members of the masters' union, the Manufacturers' Association. However, at meeting with the union weavers it was pointed out, 'in a friendly way', that if they refused work on contracts from manufacturers involved in the dispute, members of the union would not get any new work at Starkeys' so long as the strike lasted.[8]

Expansion and modernization of the mill continued. In 1841 a mill and dyehouse at the other side of the canal were acquired from Thomas Blackburne. When an inventory of machinery was made in 1857 it was still referred to as 'Blackburne's Mill' and used for fulling. The 'Old Mill', 'Low End Mill' and 'Top End Mill' are also mentioned. In 1841 the right was granted by Huddersfield Canal Co. to erect buildings along 180 yards of the towpath wall. Alterations were certainly taking place in

1849 when a mason found a hoard of 294 sovereigns during demolition. Following the death of Thomas Starkey a new partnership was established with George Brook, 'for many years' cashier and confidential clerk to firm, (not to be confused with the sacked socialist!). His son, Thomas Walker Brook, later undertook much of the running of the mill along with John Starkey's son, Lewis Randle Starkey. George died in 1884. In 1894 the firm become a limited company and the premises were renamed Springdale Mills.[9]

Thomas Brook, in evidence to the 1875 Parliamentary Committee on the LNWR and the canal, stated that in the last ten years £60,000 had been spent on the mill, which now employed 700 workers. During the alterations in 1869 the *Huddersfield Examiner* claimed that the largest block of stone ever brought to Huddersfield, 11ft 6in by 9ft by 2ft and weighing 15 tons, had been transported by Charles Holt's traction engine to make a bed for a new horizontal engine at the mill. Four years later Holt summonsed Brook, claiming he had not received money for work done between 1868 and 1872 on the boiler house. A steam economizer, engine and boiler made by Galloway & Sons costing £2,650 had been installed, plus £2,500-worth of gearing. Although he was the consulting engineer and not an architect, Holt was contracted for £1,000 to make a plan for the boiler house. He also agreed to arrange the sale of the old engine and boilers. Brook said he had not been paid because he had come up with an elaborate design like the boiler house at Saltaire! Further work was carried out in 1887

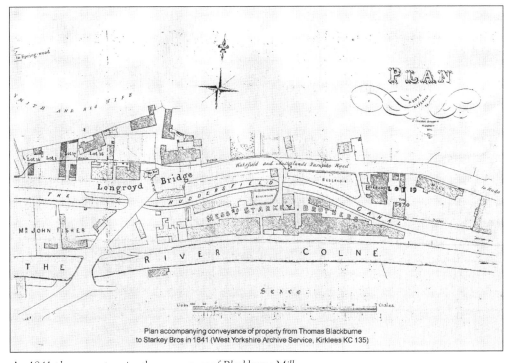

Plan accompanying conveyance of property from Thomas Blackburne to Starkey Bros in 1841 (West Yorkshire Archive Service, Kirklees KC 135)

An 1841 plan accompanying the conveyance of Blackburne Mill.

The Boiler House in 1868.

when E.W. Lockwood, architect of Byram Arcade, advertised for tenders.[10]

The firm continued to pioneer innovations. In 1888 they tried out fire-resistant screens between the scribblers to limit circulation of fluff and, in 1896, patent improvements in the method of and apparatus for consuming smoke in steam boiler furnaces. A representative of Starkey's went in 1905 on a local manufacturers delegation to mills at Gladbach in Germany to see revolutionary carding machines at work.[11]

For such a large mill with so many employees remarkably few accidents are recorded. In 1874 a twenty-one-year-old female from Berry Brow was injured and in 1895 Joe Bailey, a whitewasher aged twenty-seven, received fatal injuries when his clothing caught in a revolving shaft. It took two to three minutes to stop the engine before he could be cut free.[12]

The mill experienced at least four fires in its life: in 1840, 1860 and two in 1904. Disaster was narrowly averted in the last case when a more serious one broke out in a block of the mill, housing spinning and carding machines. Helped by the corporation fire engine, *Phyllis*, which had to aim the hose from across the canal, damage was limited to two floors and a large quantity of cloth was rescued by the workers. The mill was working day and night at the time on a contract for cloth for the Japanese army, then engaged in the war against Russia.[13]

But Starkey Bros' days were numbered. On 15 March 1907 Springdale Mill closed down. The premises and machinery were auctioned by George Tinker & Sons, the looms in particular realising very high prices, with even fifteen-year-old ones fetching £30 each. Among the buildings were included a 550-square yard weaving shed and seven multi-storey mills, which had been powered by five Galloway boilers running two horizontal condensing engines. The local socialist paper *The Worker* expressed concern for the hundreds of employees who had lost their jobs, many too old to find work elsewhere, commenting: 'Country estates have been bought, commissions in the Army purchased, parliamentary elections have been both lost and won, day schools have been built and a church opposite the mill erected and all these and the other accompaniments to wealth and position have accrued from the profits of the mills.' Any doubts about this opinion must have been dispelled by the death in 1910 of Lewis Starkey, now of Norwood Park, Southwell, Nottinghamshire, leaving a gross estate valued at the then massive sum of £200,310.[15]

Springdale Mill was leased by a number of different firms, (at least six occupying the premises in 1910) and subsequently underwent many changes of use. All the buildings, which had for so long dominated Longroyd Bridge like a moated fortress between canal and Colne, were finally levelled to the ground in the early 1980s. St Thomas' church still stands as a reminder of the Starkey family, but the mill, the monument to the thousands of local people who laboured in its shadow, has disappeared without a trace.[16]

Acknowledgements

Thanks to the staff of Huddersfield Local History Library and Kirklees Archive Service for help during this research.
For end notes please see pp. 85-86.

Alan J. Brooke

A sales advertisement and plan, 1907.

Scholars and Schoolteachers: Education in Kirkheaton

'Education, education, education'. It has always been in the news. Alterations are constantly being made to the way schools are run to improve results. But has anything really changed?

In the seventeenth century a grammar school was opened in Kirkheaton, linked as most early schools were to the Church, since clerics were one of the minority groups who could read and write. It providing an education for some of the local youngsters but few were lucky enough to attend. By the age of three or four, most would be working around their home, responsible for looking after animals, or picking stones from the fields – anything which would earn a few pence.

Not until the nineteenth century was it realized that education was needed for all if the 'workshop of the world' was going to maintain its lead and have a skilled workforce. In 1845 the old grammar school was replaced by a National School. The old buildings were demolished and new ones built, spreading on to the extra land given by the Beaumonts of Whitley. A reflection of the times is shown in the comment that the land was to be: 'appropriated and used as and for a school for the education of children and adults, or children only of the labouring, manufacturing or other poorer classes in the parish of Kirkheaton,.

The cost, £1643 13s 7d, was raised mainly by donations with small grants from the National Society and government. In 1872 an infants'

73

Cross Mill during demolition, 1982-83.

department opened, moving to its own site in Field Rise in 1883. By 1913 an extension was needed but the building ceased to function as a school in 1966.

But schools are not just buildings, education is not just a series of subjects to be learned. It involves the people who go to the schools, the people who teach there and the local community. So who did go to that local school? This is the story of some of the people there at the end of Victoria's reign.

In 1873 the head teacher was Henry Whiteley, a local man from Linthwaite. The log books he wrote show a fascinating picture of life in a Victorian school and the beginning of our education system. As well as the Master, there was an assistant mistress and four pupil teachers. Senior pupils were taught to read, then helped teach the younger pupils. This was a cheap method but Henry Whiteley was already questioning its use – he comments that it works well but prevents progress by the older ones. The most promising pupils, if their families could afford and would agree, were taken on as pupil teachers, some then going on to college for formal training.

The other teachers in 1879 included Florence Broadbent, the assistant teacher, who left shortly after this to work in Conisbrough. Pupil teachers were Alfred Liversedge, Lee Wilson, the son of a local farmer; Florence Stocks and Betty Cliffe whose fathers were pattern weavers. Later they were joined by Thomas Hey, who had been a pupil at the school, also the son of a weaver, and Richard Canby. Richard's father was the local police constable, though whether this helped Richard keep order or made matters worse is not recorded.

It was not just the pupils who had to

study. Pupil teachers had their lessons before and after school, and the Head often observed their lessons, explaining faults afterwards. Exams then had to be taken to show their progress. Serious fault was found with one set of papers and the girl had to explain that as she was looking at the papers a 'dimness came over her eyes'. The master confirmed that she generally did work hard so this was accepted as a genuine case! Sometimes the pupil teachers got an extra holiday. In 1881 they were given a day's leave to go to Bradford to see the Prince of Wales. This must have been a special occasion for them – a journey all the way to Bradford, the excitement of the crowd, not to mention a day off work.

But there were problems to deal with. One pupil teacher, Miss Taylor, had a number of absences through the 'illness and death of her mother'. Soon after this, she left to take up a new appointment in London. Two years later, Thomas Hey had time off because of his father's death and found it difficult to settle back to his duties because his sister was also dangerously ill. It was not unusual for a family to suffer a number of bereavements one after the other. He did eventually settle down and went on to Cheltenham to take his exams, before leaving, with his fellow pupil teacher, Richard Canby, to go to teacher training college. Pupil teacher Lee Wilson had gone previously to York Teacher Training College for his exam, but had been refused on the grounds of ill health. He had obviously worked hard at the school, though, since they took him on the staff anyway.

Then, as now, inspections caused considerable stress in the school. Specified standards had to be reached in order to receive the government grant. In

Kirkheaton School.

July 1879, 280 pupils out of a possible 286 took their 'standard' exams; classes were divided into Standards I to VI and children were expected to pass one standard before moving upwards. Some never moved! The exams for Standard I, for six and seven-year-olds, included the ability to 'read a short paragraph from a book not confined to words of one syllable', while by Standard IV (the normal leaving age) children of thirteen were expected to be able to 'read with intelligence'. Some lucky few were able to stay at school long enough to reach Standard VI when they could 'read with fluency and expression.' Writing and arithmetic were also covered by these Standards.

One inspection reported that reading was below par and geography results were poor, but 'penmanship, needlework and singing were carefully taught'. More modern comments include the fact that spelling needed attention, the children did not speak clearly enough, were fidgety and 'far too noisy out of school'. The Master decided to take action: 'To avoid noise the children have been required to march in and out of school on tiptoe.' In clogs and wooden soled shoes this must have taken some skill – it would have been much easier for those who were unable to afford any shoes at all.

It was sad to see the comment in a later paragraph of the log book: 'Hamby Adams who took the Standard II exam on Wednesday last is reported dead this morning of an inflammation.' Doctors had to be paid for and often had little idea how to cure their patients. Other diseases also occurred and caused problems for the school. In April 1880 one child arrived and informed the Master that her brother had the measles. She 'was immediately sent home'. By May, Henry Whiteley was recording that attendance was low because of measles and scarlet fever in the village.

It was important to record reasons for absence as this could be used to explain pupils not progressing fast enough. Some pupils are described as 'half-timers'. Not pupils truanting as they do today (although there were plenty of those too), but children working, legally, part-time. Reference is frequently made to the effect of these 'half-timers' and headmaster Whiteley decided eventually to reorganize some of his classes into full-timers and half-timers, rather than Standards IV to VI. In this way he hoped to prevent the half-timers holding back the others. At the same time, he also dropped the teaching of needlework, teaching grammar instead as it was easier to set homework for the half-timers.

Many of us still like to give the house a good 'spring clean' and the same applied in the nineteenth century. The Kirkheaton school log books record that 'cleaning down at home has begun and this will affect the attendance until Whitsuntide'. Spring cleaning took a long time – carpets had to be taken outside and beaten to get rid of the winter's accumulation of dirt, washed curtains would take a long time to dry. It is noticeable that this causes the girls attendance problems – not boys!

Despite the limitations of teacher training, practitioners were beginning to question how to get the best out of their pupils. Whiteley comments on the small rewards he gave for map drawing which produced 'some capital work'. He goes on to query 'Would small rewards frequently

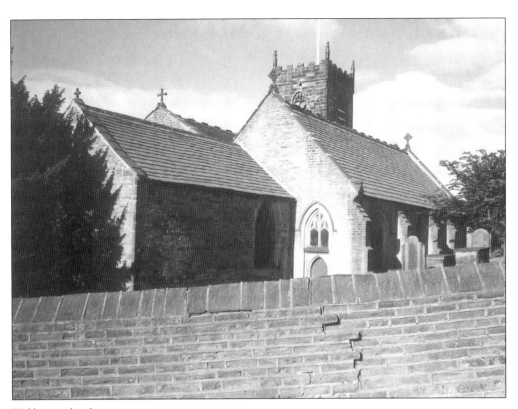

Kirkheaton church.

given produce better results than annual prizes?' Whatever his private conclusions, the school continued to give a variety of annual prizes, not just for good work but for regular and punctual attendance as well. Places were allocated in classes for this and the headmaster comments that few children were late as they would then lose their place. Medals were given too. The prizes were distributed at an evening event – though only a few parents attended – with the Rector giving the certificates and medals.

Not all the children were angels. The cane was allowed, though not by assistant teachers. There is evidence that this was, on occasions, abused. Mr Brown used the cane 'severely' and his employment was not continued. The teacher of Standard I was also warned about this after complaints from parents. However, poorly behaved children had to be dealt with. Willie Roebuck received two strokes of the cane for 'rudeness to the vicar'. Unfortunately, he didn't receive this punishment well but 'muttered something and walked off home'. His father was asked to come to school next day! Others were dealt with more severely. Harry Liversedge was expelled, being described as 'the dread of teachers and of little boys...' There were other hazards to contend with. The game of whip top became the craze and 'trouble caused both in and out of school with the whips'.

An early form to 'Citizenship' was

taught in order to improve behaviour. Lessons on politeness and good manners included: 'Entrance into and departure from school room; Ditto as to stranger's house; On the use of 'Thank You' and 'If You Please'; On giving way to the wishes of others; The readiness to assist others, whether the wants be made known or observed only; On respect to superiors.' There are some standards which should, perhaps, be revived!

But not all school life was hard work. Henry Whiteley 'allowed children to peruse a few numbers of the *Illustrated London News* out of school hours. The older children seem much pleased and no doubt will be benefited by a continuance of the plan.' A half day's holiday was given to witness the laying of the corner stone for the new Infants' School, and by 1885 a school library was established, though the principal decision was which cupboard to use, so it was not extensive. Shakespeare, Milton, Shelley and Chaucer were included, while prose reading consisted of Gibbon's *Decline and Fall of the Roman Empire* and Scott's *Ivanhoe*. They also had the equivalent of today's 'numeracy hour', but at that time it was a 'regulation on mental arithmetic' and consisted of ten minutes' repetition of tables, etc. This was put to good use when the Inspectors arrived and asked the pupils questions such as this: 'The daily wages of 2 men and 5 women together equal 32 shillings. If each man's wage exceeds a woman's by 2 shillings, find out the rate of pay for each.' Most pupils nowadays would cite the Equal Pay Act! (The answer is that the men got 6s and the women 4s.)

Visitors were a regular part of the school day. Local 'top' families often appeared to see how the children were progressing, and the school had close links with the Church. The children attended services there and the vicar helped teach Scripture in the school.

The school year must have passed quite quickly. Autumn term then, as now, welcomed new pupils who would have to learn the school rules. Winter brought bad weather and poor attendance as pupils were unable to travel or were ill from poor nutrition. Spring brought more outdoor nature walks and object lessons, whilst summer saw the leaving of children who, having passed Standard IV and reached the age of thirteen were free to leave. Summer was also the time when inspectors arrived to examine the pupils – a worrying time. Too few passes and the school grant was cut. Summer also brought the holidays, but only three weeks before autumn term began again.

Many of the pupils were born, lived, worked and eventually died in the Kirkheaton or Huddersfield area. Most would find employment in the local mills or mines where the majority of their parents already worked. But for a few the education received at Kirkheaton school provided them with a way to a better future than their parents had known, with more opportunities, more expertise and the ability to learn new skills needed for the coming twentieth century. In some ways, not much has changed in education, has it?

Bibliography
1881 Census records, Huddersfield.
Brooke, J.M., *The Story of Three Schools* (Kirklees Reference Library).
Chapman, C.R., *The Growth of British Education and its Records* (Lochin Publishing)

Log books of Kirkheaton National School 1879-93, Kirklees Archives, ref No E/KH/PR 9/2/1.

May, T., *The Victorian Schoolroom* (Shire Publications Ltd).

Valerie Teasdale

Last of the Summer Wine Country

Whenever I hear a brass band playing, especially on a summer's day, when the sound is carried on a gentle breeze, my mind is instantly transported back to the days when I was a child. Hepworth Band used to practise in the old mill at the bottom of our road. Whenever the sun came out, so did they, into the mill yard, carrying with them little old chairs. They would assemble, then practise their music. They were a first-class band and prize winners. The band practice day was my mother's baking day. So, in my memory I can smell newly baked bread and visualize the little thimble cakes made just for me, custards and pasties, all looking most delectable. Not only that, it was brewing day, as well. From the young nettles we had gathered on our walks mother would brew nettle beer. The sparkle and taste of it was out of this world. I can also smell the new-mown hay and see it straggling on the ground, clinging to the stones where it had fallen off the hay cart. My father used to help the farmer and seemed to enjoy it – possibly for the scrumptious ham and eggs that followed – for a job well done. Those days seemed full of sunshine, timeless and long. The evenings were wonderful, warm

Leading Wren Haigh (the author).

and magical. We longed to stay in that atmosphere, afraid that the spell would be broken if we went to bed too soon.

The Village of Hepworth

Hepworth is a very pretty village 750ft above sea level. It has kept its character throughout the years – apart from the occasional new houses it remains the same. The only change is that the cobbled streets have been replaced with tarmac.

In days long ago most of the cottages were used for weaving – they have a great many windows for light. Also there were several farms. Another type of work was mining; there were many pits. Children and women used to work in the mines in the nineteenth century. Eventually the Co-operative movement began. Local people put their savings together and

The communal grave from the days of the plague, never to be touched.

started a Co-op. It was in two cottages down Main Gate. My cottage, 72 Main Gate, is where the public entered. It moved to larger premises on Town Gate in 1840.

Hepworth has many Biblical names. We have the 'Vale of Jordan' – through this wood runs a stream, which, as long as I can remember, contained trout. The 'Garden of Paradise' is a small but lovely compact garden, just off Town Gate. 'Solomon's Temple' is a cottage, which stands on its own, on the right near the lych gate of the church. It has a lovely atmosphere: 'Hades', meaning Hadedge, is half a mile away. Other unusual names are 'Meal Hill', 'Donkey Lane', 'Cuckoo Steps', 'Larks House', 'Barnside' and 'Gatehead'.

'Larks House' is where all the hounds were kept. When I was a child, the hounds were trained very well. They had to go on a long walk before breakfast and were not allowed to do their business. If any young ones attempted, they were tapped with the Huntsman's whip. On their arrival back at the kennels they would all pass excrement which was duly scraped up and put into drums. These were collected and paid for and went to a firm in Halifax (which eventually put the sheen on leather).

Also at Larks House, parts of pigs and sheep – offal, pigs' snouts – would all be chopped up and were sold to make into jellies!! The skins of sheep were sold for rugs, the small pieces made into wash-leathers after special treatment. Not many people were aware of this.

The End of the Plague

Our band used to lead the procession for Hepworth Feast. This was always the first Monday after 28 June, to commemorate the end of the plague in 1665. The village was almost wiped out; people had to bury their own dead at midnight.

How we eagerly awaited this day of days – it was extra-special. I was usually dressed all in white. We used to walk round the village and stop at the same set points every year. We sang hymns, the favourites being 'Summer suns are glowing over land and sea', 'Guide me, O thou great Jehovah', 'In loving kindness Jesus came', 'Sun of my soul, thou Saviour dear', 'Jesus shall reign where'er the sun', 'God be with you till we meet again'. Which reminds me – Sir John Betjeman on his way to Derbyshire missed his way and came down Foster Place and then called at Hepworth Chapel. He loved the stained glass window depicting Mary with baby Jesus and above two angels guarding them.

When we had done the route we would all

rush up to the Sunday School for sandwiches, biscuits and buns, washed down with strong hot tea from the gleaming copper urns. Afterwards we would join a queue where we were presented with school cakes. We would grab our cakes then shoot home to join an endless stream of visitors. We would sit down with them at the table and always finish up with strawberries and cream. At 6.30 everyone congregated in the village where once more we would join the band and go through the hymn sheet. When completed, we would follow the band into the gala field.

The next move – we would stare wide-eyed at the over-flowing sweet stall. I usually ended up with 'gob stoppers' periodically taking them out of my mouth to see the change of colour. My next delight would be to have a Kaly with a liquorice stick to dip in and lick feverishly. A 'lucky bag' would be my next choice. Fascinated by the unknown, my hands trembled as I opened it, expecting a priceless treasure of some kind. I was always disappointed, for it usually contained tasteless sweets.

My Village

I must have been very young but one day my mother put a dress on me that looked familiar. Then I remembered: I had seen my elder sister wearing it. The snag was it fitted me as a dress – my sister's jumper. There it was running around in my brain like an old cracked record. I was so ashamed, I tried to hide. This early recollection still sends a wave of dread over me, as I remember trying to swallow my pride. Shortage of money always seemed to be the problem at our house. I used to think people who were rich were bound to be happy.

It was customary for children in our village to wear clogs, as they were very hard-wearing. They only required what was known as ironing occasionally. They were tipped at the soles and heels with steel over a wooden base with uppers of leather. I thought, 'Heaven forbid, 1 don't want any clogs'. My worst fears came to pass. One day my little clogs arrived. Although they were put on my feet very gently I screamed and screamed. 'Take them off, they are hurting me'. I choked as tears ran down my cheeks. They were hastily removed. Where did they hurt? All the family were concerned. I took a quick breath as I said warily, watching their expressions from out of my eye corners 'The sides of my feet'. The truth was, it was my pride that was hurt. I wanted to wear shoes. Clogs were for poor working classes. How upsetting it was for me to know that every penny counted. To see the strain on the faces of Mum and Dad. Yet I wanted shoes so much. 'Well' Dad said, 'We'll have to make a special effort for t'child's sake. Clogs would cripple her, especially when she has such sensitive feet.' My Dad said bravely, 'She'll get her shoes if I have to go without bacca for a week.' Yes, I got my shoes, and none know of my little white lie. I was the baby in those days, a weakling at birth. The doctor pursed his lips as he said quietly, 'Is she to her time?' I was born with bronchitis and a weak heart. I took a lot of rearing (and was christened on the rug by Philip Lovell Snowden).

Hepworth House was a big house that overlooked our cottage. One day, when the doctor called on the two old ladies they told him that the child down Main Gate was dead. He wasn't a bit surprised. As he arrived at our house Mum was just drawing the curtains, so he knew how the mistake had occurred. What had kept me alive was whisky. My lips were kept moist with it. My mother was not very robust and whilst carrying me she had lived on butter biscuits.

One day, she overheard some neighbours talking as she was hanging out the washing 'Ee, she must be strong,' said one. Little knowing that she was hanging on to the clothes line for support. She was too proud to ask for help and couldn't afford to pay anyone. So we struggled through the best we could.

The Co-op

To me, one of the most important places was the Co-op. I loved to go there. It was the highlight of my day. It was customary for children to run errands; it never ever entered our heads to refuse. We were brought up to help and respect the elderly. For returning a

half-pound empty glass jam jar you would be paid a halfpenny, for a two-pound jar one penny, or you could have sweets. There were several assistants; my favourite was the under manager, called Joe. He was a shy, chubby-faced man inclined to be forgetful. I always waited my opportunity, standing in the background until he could serve me. As I sidled up to him he would say 'What song are we practising today, then?' He was a good musician and played the violin. So whilst he was filling a huge bag of sweets for me we would be talking about singing. When the bag was almost full to overflowing I would scoop it up and quickly, like a butterfly, be out of the shop leaving Joe singing, looking up to the

The favourite stained glass window which Sir John Betjeman loved: baby Jesus on his mother's lap, guarded by angels.

beautiful hills – 'Oh for the Wings of a Dove' was always his choice.

'Divi Day' was quite a celebration. Everyone had a cheque number and had to join a queue. This was a great day; everyone would be looking important. They would peep at the slip, then put their hand over the total so that no-one else could see. Usually this was the money that bought our new clothes. Otherwise I doubt whether we should have had any.

I used to love to go upstairs where the pots and pans were kept. Such an array of splendour to me. Also, the room next to it was the corn chamber where the big crane hauled up big boxes of soap, potatoes and bags of flour. It fascinated me. I never tired of tripping up to that attic; it was full of magic and mystery to me. The cellar was also interesting. This contained large stone slabs where the vinegar kegs and barrels of treacle were stored. It had many unusual arches and little alcoves, which were most enchanting. My eyes like a camera lens zoomed on, clicking instant pictures for my memory bank. I can still smell the freshness of white Windsor soap. For each pound you bought you were given a 'free towel wrapper'. For twelve wrappers you received a lovely free towel.

I can still see the young shop assistants chatting jovially to each other as they packed groceries in large cardboard brown boxes, to be delivered to the farmsteads on the hills. 'Come on, Muriel,' they would say, 'give us a song'. They asked for 'There are Fairies at the Bottom of our Garden'. 'At least,' they would plead, 'Sing summat'.

The only thing I disliked about the Co-op was the butchers. How I hated Mondays. As this terrible memory unfolds I can hear the animals screaming. The butcher, in those days, actually killed the animals. Hidden deep in my mind dwells the squeals of terror which penetrated to my heart. Animals in those days were not killed in a humane way, if killing can ever come under the heading as 'humane'. I used to try and cover my ears to shut out their cries. Bullocks were first of all tied tightly with a rope through a metal ring, then held tightly at each end so that they couldn't possibly escape. They were then hit on the head with a mallet type of hammer. Inside was concealed a long pointed like knife that penetrated through the skull. Pigs had their throats slit. Some looked so young it made my heart ache as they ran up the yard. They were, I am sure, squealing for their mother.

My brother and his mates used to hang about until it was all over. They were waiting for the pig's bladder to use as a football. I still shudder at the thought. I can still hear their agonising groans and feel I could choke with the nauseating stench and smell of blood that prevailed nearby. Such a sad memory lying in the corner of my mind.

But I remember too, the manager, Robert Bedford. His hair and moustache were white and strong. He had a thin pale face and brown eyes and always spoke very quietly. He was what I call a real gentleman. Joe, his only brother, was exactly opposite having a full round face with pink pouchy cheeks and blue eyes. His hair was fair, very thin and silky. However, they had one thing in common. They were both good conscientious workers. They would stay up all night if only a halfpenny was missing, until it was accounted for. They were wonderful people. Later, when I started going to musical festivals Joe would tag along with us.

My Mother

My mother had little to sing about, yet she sang all day long. Her beautiful soprano voice could be heard from dawn to dusk. Favourites were 'When Will the Sun Shine for Me?',

'Silver Threads mongst the Gold', 'I Wonder If You'll Miss Me Sometime'. She also loved hymns, her favourite being 'The Old Rugged Cross'. Her supply was endless and her voice was renowned throughout the neighbourhood. She was an attractive woman, very much like the Queen Mother. She also had good taste; her speciality was hats and she loved unusual styles. In spite of not having much money she always looked smart and smelt of fragrant perfume. She was a good housewife and often helped others with their housework. For this she received a pittance. Even so, it helped to pay the bills. She hated drinking or any intoxicants. My dad never had much spending money but when he had been out with his mates he invariably came back the worse for beer. Mother used to get very upset and would natter.

How I used to hate these rows. I used to go to bed and put my hands over my ears to try and shut it out. When these scenes occurred I worried and cried a lot. I suppose that is why I always looked pale and drawn. We all hated these days, yet said very little as our loyalties were divided.

Mum also made rugs and they were really beautiful. How we all loved to walk on them in our bare feet. She also did all the decorating. The pennies spent on the paper looked as if it had cost pounds. The house ceiling was wood and she loved to scrub it. Oh, how proud she was if someone called and commented on it. Yes, both our parents were good hardworking people, in fact the salt of the earth. They helped everyone and anyone, getting little thanks for their pains. Yet they always said, it is better to do a good turn than a bad one. This was their code of life. 'You'll never find better people than us,' my parents used to say. I thought whatever do they mean? Are they living in a delusion? We had very little money and little education. These two factors, I thought, meant everything. The people who had these attributes therefore received respect and good positions, which I thought were the main things in life. The people who possess them had everything. How wrong I was. As I grew older I realised my parents' words were true, there were no better people. Having money and education makes life easier but it says nothing for their character. In fact, on the whole these two important points have made not good reliable people but a lot of criminals. They put their education and brains into making yet more money through false pretences, so therefore were not to be envied.

Mum and Dad were also true to each other and kept their marriage vows. I know this to be true because children are very perceptive. As I said previously, money, or rather lack of it, caused a lot of worry and heartache. One day Mum said to Dad, 'I know what I'm going to do.' Dad looked up from a pile of horse magazines 'What's that?' Mum drew herself up to her full height and said, 'I'm going to leave you'. Dad looked horrified and his face was white. I and my sisters and brother never said a word. Suddenly Dad said, 'Well, you'll do summat worse 'n that'. 'Oh, and what's that?' said Mum haughtily. 'Well, you'll atta come back.' Too true, the ice was broken and we all had a laugh. You see there was nowhere to run to; we had to cope and carry on as best we could.

Muriel Kelly

End notes

The Eland Feud

[1] For an example of how the traditional interpretation of the feud is still used today, see the Internet site, 'Malcolm Bull's Trivia Trail' at www.halifax-today/specialfeatures/triviatrail/mme50.html.

[2] *Calendar of Patent Rolls 1348-1350*, vol. 8, and *Calendar of Patent Rolls 1350-1354*, vol. 9 [henceforward *CPR* and date] (Nendeln/Liechtenstein, 1971); the Records of the King's Bench are extensively discussed in J.M. Kaye, 'The Eland Murders, 1350-51: A Study of the Legend of the Eland Feud', *The Yorkshire Archaeological Journal*, **51** (1979), pp. 61-79; M. O'Regan & B. Hale (eds), *The Court Rolls of the Manor of Wakefield from October 1350 to September 1352* (Yorkshire Archaeological Society, 1987), and H.M. Jewell (ed.), *The Court Rolls of the Manor of Wakefield from September 1348 to September 1350* (Yorkshire Archaeological Society, 1981) [henceforward *Court Rolls* and date].

[3] The version used here is published in J. Watson, *The History and Antiquities of the Parish of Halifax in Yorkshire* (London, 1775), pp. 172-176.

[4] Kaye, *op. cit.*, pp. 77-78.

[5] The date of the Tourn does not correspond with the date of Sir John's death. Kaye, *op. cit.*, p. 67.

[6] *Ibid.*, p. 64.

[7] Stanza 77.

[8] Kaye, *op. cit.*, p. 69.

[9] *CPR 1350-1354*, p. 156.

[10] Stanzas 16, 17, 24 & 93; Watson, *op. cit.*, p. 178; T. Dyson, *The History of Huddersfield and District*, 2nd ed. (Huddersfield, 1951), p. 125.

[11] See Appendix 1; also Stanzas 15 & 23.

[12] Kaye, *op. cit.*, p. 73.

[13] 'Dodsworth's Note of the Feud between Eland and Beaumont, MS cxlv, f107', *The Yorkshire Archaeological Journal*, **2** (1873), Appendix 1, p. 163; T. Dyson, *op. cit.* p. 124-127.

[14] Stanzas 31 & 58.

[15] Kaye, *op. cit.*, pp. 67 & 71.

[16] *Court Rolls 1348-1350*; *Court Rolls 1350-1352*.

[17] Kaye, *op. cit.*

[18] Quoted in Kaye, *op. cit.*, p. 64.

[19] Kaye, *op. cit.*, pp. 64 & 68.

[20] *Ibid.*, p. 67.

[21] Appendix 1; *CPR 1354-1358*, p. 592; Kaye, *op. cit.*, p. 64.

[22] Kaye, *op. cit.*, pp. 64, 74-75.

[23] *Ibid.*, p. 64.

[24] Appendix 1.

[25] Appendix 2.

[26] Kaye, *op. cit.*, p. 64.

[27] Dyson, *op. cit.*, p. 144; W. Paley Baildon (ed.), 'The Eland Feud', *Yorkshire Archaeological Journal*, **11** (1891), p. 128.

[28] *Court Rolls 1348-1350*, pp. 231, 236 & 238; *Court Rolls 1350-1352*, pp. 82 & 97.

[29] *Court Rolls 1348-1350*, pp. 34, 61, 69 & 228.

Starkey's Mill

[1] Directory, 1822, 1830; for the date of the original mill, see *Factory Commissioners' Report*, 1834; Thomas Walker Brook, 'Parliamentary Committee on LNWR', in *Huddersfield Examiner* (HE), 15 May 1874; *The Worker*, 16 March 1907.

[2] *Leeds Times* (LT), 21 February & 9 May 1835; HE, 2 April 1853.

[3] LT, 21 February & 9 May 1835; HE, 2 April 1853; D.T. Jenkins, *The West Riding Wool Industry 1770-1835* (Pasold, 1975), pp. 166-168; for a reconstruction see Royal Commission for Historic Monuments, *Yorkshire Textile Mills 1770-1930* (HMSO, 1992), p. 102.

[4] *Voice of the West Riding*, 27 July, 23 November, 28 December 1833; *Pioneer*, 1 March 1834; *HE*, 15 January 1881; obituary for George Brook, *LT*, 14 & 21 December 1839; *New Moral World*, 28 June 1845; *Leeds Mercury (LM)*, 20 August 1842.

[5] *LM*, 13 April, 4 May 1844, 30 September 1848; *HE*, 2 April 1853, 31 March 1860.

[6] S. Chadwick, 'The Starkeys and their Church', in *HE*, 30 August 1975; D.F.E. Sykes, *History of Huddersfield*, p. 149; *LM*, 29 May 1847, 13 October 1849, 6 April 1850; *HE*, 31 July 1852.

[7] *Huddersfield Chronicle (HC)*, 5 January 1861, 14 June 1862, 14 March 1863; *HE*, 24 January 1874; *Huddersfield Weekly News*, 18 April 1891; *Yorkshire Factory Times (YFT)*, 18 January 1895.

[8] *HE*, 17 March 1883.

[9] West Yorkshire Archive Service, Kirklees, KC.135; *LM*, 30 January 1849; obituary for T.W. Brook, in *HE*, 31 January 1903. The name Springdale first occurs in the 1897 *White's Directory*.

[10] *HE*, 10 July 1869, 12 April 1873, 15 May 1875 (Brook explained that the mill relied on water from the canal for its operations), 29 July 1887.

[11] *HE*, 3 November 1888, 16 May 1896.

[12] *HE*, 11 April 1874; *YFT*, 18 January 1895.

[13] *LM*, 17 April 1841; *HC*, 12 May 1860; *HE*, 19 July, 15 October 1904.

[14] *The Worker*, 16 March, 27 April 1837, 28 January 1911; KC.135 sales advetisement and plan.

[15] *Yorkshire Textile Directory* 1910 *et seq*.

CHAPTER 3
Memories

Marjorie Fleur Oldfield in the twenties.

Childhood

When I was eight, for many reasons which I was not aware of at the time, I lived with my maternal Grandma, whom I loved very dearly. In fact she was more like my mother than my grandmother. Her little cottage in Upper Slades, Yorkshire, was just two rooms and an outhouse, where she did her washing. There was a dolly-tub and posser, rubbing board and boiler to heat the water, and a stone floor of course.

Washing day was a long process as the sheets and all whites had to be boiled. The soap was hard and had to be cut into shreds so they would melt easier in the water. Then they were dolly-blued. This came from a little bag and when whites were dipped into the mixture it produced, they really did become whiter. Many items had to be starched as women wore a lot of petticoats in those days. Washing took nearly all day, so Grandma made a quick dinner, made up of the Sunday joint and potatoes called 'hash'. It was very tasty and cheap; meat was inexpensive in those days, so there was always a joint on Sunday whatever happened.

Her living room/kitchen had a Yorkshire range, a fire in the middle with a boiler at one side and an oven at the other. This was the only means of heating water and cooking Grandma had. Yet she baked all her own bread, scones and cooked dishes such as steak and kidney pie, roast beef, Yorkshire pudding and custard tart etc. As I hated fruit in cakes Grandma made some with caraway seeds in just for me; these days they are like bits of grit in my denture-filled mouth!

Downstairs in Grandma's cottage a highly polished table stood in the centre of the room, which was kept covered with a thick tablecloth. I still have a tiny piece of it after fifty years. A horsehair sofa, which was very prickly when sat on, and a few hard-backed chairs were the seating arrangements. The only form of lighting came from gas mantles. Many times Mother, being tall, would break it with her head by knocking against it when she called to see us. A wind-up gramophone was the only form of music there. Her two records from the *Tales of Hoffman* were played so often that I grew to hate them to the extent of throwing a tantrum.

The first film I ever saw was when Grandma took me to the local cinema to see Al Jolson in *The Singing Fool*. When his little son died, how we both wept and wept! He sang 'Climb upon my Knee Sonny Boy' very movingly.

Grandma never saw another film, for not long after she became ill. Dropsy was what they called it in those days. She grew very fat. I had to help her up the steep stairs to bed, one foot at a time. I disliked doing this for some reason, but I was very small and young. The big brass bed dominated the room, with frilly lacy hangings which she had crocheted herself. The feather mattress was so deep it nearly hid me from sight, and how cosy it was on winter nights when the wind howled round the house. To this day I love the sound of the wind ... it reminds me of Grandma.

From the tiny window in the bedroom I could see right across the valley to the railway lines. I loved to watch the steam trains puffing their way to London or Manchester. I had never been on a train at that time. Our brief outings were by motor coach to Blackpool or Scarborough. It took nearly all day to get there.

Grandma, being left a widow with six children, never went out, even before she became ill. I felt sorry when my Auntie Dorothy told me they could never have books except at Christmas when they had the usual annuals, they were so poor.

At last Grandma died; I'll never forget the day they buried her. It was a black day in every way. The sky was black with thunderclouds, the horses were black, and all the relatives and pallbearers wore black. Not only were the horses black, they had black plumes on their heads. The ladies' handkerchiefs were edged with black lace. Only we children were allowed to wear any other colour. It took eight men to lift the coffin into the hearse as she was so heavy at this time. The churchyard was muddy and the rain fell heavily. Mother told me to throw a small bunch of flowers on the top of the coffin, so I did. I said good-bye to Grandma and life was never the same again.

I was taken ill with kidney trouble soon afterwards, and Auntie Dorothy has since told me that I nearly died. When I had recovered a little, I had to rest quietly on Auntie's sofa and watch her at her tasks around the house. If I kept asking questions she would say in dialect, 'Tha war na wiz'. Although I had no idea what this meant I could tell by the tone of her voice that she was cross, so I never asked. Auntie never spoke in dialect except when she was annoyed, so if I kept asking 'What are you doing Auntie?' she would say crossly 'Ahm makking wimwams for ducks to pe-ak on'. I'd lived on milk for so long that one day Auntie made me a delicious meat and potato pie. The meat and gravy were so good and the crust so golden, I have never tasted such a pie since.

Auntie's daughter, cousin Phyllis, was a little tomboy, not afraid of anything or anybody. When warned that a newly acquired cockerel was rather fierce and she had better watch out for him, she said scornfully, 'I'm not frightened of a silly old hen,' and off she went to the outside toilet. Of course, the cockerel pecked her leg and she ran in crying to her mother who said 'I told you to watch out' then gave her a cuddle and one of her home made toffees. Phyllis was soon back to her normal self.

I still remember very clearly going to Uncle Oswin's. It was milking time when I got to Uncle Oswin's small farm. I must have gone with a message, for I never went without an invitation, as Aunt Letitia, Uncle's wife, was very stern and always seemed cross to me. I was frightened of her, she never smiled as Uncle did.

As I went in Uncle was pulling white cotton leggings over his trousers, a white cap on his head – where it rested against the cow – and a large white apron. He looked so clean, when he saw me he grinned, and his red face lit up with pleasure. 'I'm just going to milk the cows, would you like to watch?' he asked.

'Oh yes please,' I replied. I didn't want to have to be alone with Aunt Lettuce – as I secretly called her! Uncle, picking up a large churn, led the way out the back door, across the cobbled farmyard and into the mistle where he kept the cows. He had three, and as we went they turned to gaze at us with huge brown eyes. They stood in the stalls chewing quite peacefully.

There was a warmth about the place and a smell of cattle cake which he fed the cows. In one corner – as my eyes got used to the dark – I could see a brown hen sitting on some straw with her chicks all around her.

Uncle got a three-leg milking stool and seated himself by the nearest cow and began pulling at its teats. Swish, swish, swish I heard the milk go into the churn. After a while, I asked Uncle if I could pick up one of the chicks, so he said, 'Yes, love, but we'll have to be getting back to Auntie soon, I've nearly finished.' I went to the brown hen. I held the little chick in my hand, it was so tiny, so light. I loved the little creature and after giving it a kiss I put it back as Uncle said, 'Come on love.' Before I left for home Uncle gave me a shilling and whispered, 'Don't tell your Auntie,' I ran all the way home, I had a whole shilling!

Nearly always, I stayed over Christmas at Uncle Fred's. My two cousins, Connie and Margaret, were a bit younger than me, and on Boxing Day, along with other cousins Joan, Phyllis and myself, we all looked forward to being taken by Uncle to the meet of the local hunt at Castle Hill. It seemed such a long way to us, being so young, and our little legs ached so we said: 'Can we get on a bus, Uncle?' He puffed his pipe and replied, 'Yes, if we see one,' But it being holiday time, we never did.

Once at the top Uncle went for a drink and we sat on the wall watching the red-coated huntsmen and all the hounds eager to be off, then came the 'Tally Ho!' and

Marjorie with her young son, David.

Uncle said we'd follow on foot. It seemed so exciting; we never realized that the hounds were after hares or foxes. We ran across fields, over stiles back and forth until Uncle said, 'We'll rest here, they're bound to double back this way.' They never did, so he puffed his clay pipe and then took us back home where Auntie was waiting with a delicious meal; some sort of fowl, and a roast with sprouts, roast potatoes and Yorkshire puddings. I well recall Uncle wanting a slice of bread and dripping. Auntie would scold him, saying 'Don't show me up wanting dripping, with all this to eat!'

When the meal was over and all the pots and dishes washed up and put away, we played games. One game we all liked was Forfeits. This involved answering questions and paying a forfeit if you couldn't answer. It went on until everyone had paid a forfeit, a small object such as a ring or a brooch. Then Uncle would be blindfolded and Auntie, holding up each object over his head would ask, 'What has the owner of this fine thing to do?'

Once, when it was my forfeit Auntie was holding, I was told to go to Uncle's hen run at the end of the street with his daughter Connie, and I had to milk the nanny goat and bring the milk back. The creature wouldn't keep still and we couldn't get any milk so Connie asked a pal who lived near by for some milk, just for a laugh, and took it back to her father. He was amazed and confessed he knew the goat was obstinate and said we'd done well. Connie and I giggled at our little secret. But Uncle was always playing tricks on us. On Christmas morning we were wakened early by the church choir and the prize brass band playing and singing carols. Uncle would send one of us out with a half-penny and we had to say 'do play in the next street'. Just as they were moving off, Uncle would give us a shilling to give them. It seemed like one long laugh, being at Uncle Fred's.

Marjorie Fleur Oldfield

Happy Wartime Days

They say that it's a mistake to go back to rekindle old memories, but for old times' sake I wanted to see again the school in which I spent so many happy years. As I walked up Brook Street, so familiar to me, after all these years, I recalled anxious moments, scurrying up the deserted street when I was late. Alas, there was no trace of the church school at Moldgreen, the place that shaped our lives and made a lasting impression on me so long ago.

Empire Day, 1939. We were only five and dressed up for the occasion. From left to right, back row: Margaret Hurst, Shirley Dyson, Elsie Kilvington, Dorothy Adamson, Sheila Rhodes. Middle row: ? Bottomley, Guy Gibson, -?-, Peter Longley, Geoffrey Hoyle. Front row: Pauline Jackson, -?-, -?-.

As the war progressed, we noticed the mysterious disappearance of the iron railings, gone to help the war effort, we were told. Making our way up Brook Street to school each morning, we saw the ugly stumps of iron still embedded in the walls of the little gardens; sad reminders of their former glory.

The tiny infants' school was my first step on the formal education ladder. I can still see that big rocking horse that could take three little riders at once; the piano whose back was decorated with a large frieze made out of brightly-coloured felt, depicting contrary Mary in her growing flower garden. Not for us the chance to paint every day: the large jam jars of paint came out once a week. The phrase 'Lie face downwards and take a rest' still rings in my ears.

Did we take much of a rest to the sound of the rippling piano notes? Was this part of a music and movement lesson, or merely an afternoon siesta? No doubt fearing that we war children might be under-nourished, they gave us warm Horlicks every morning, served up in lovely little beakers decorated with nursery rhyme pictures.

A memory that refuses to leave me also concerns nursery rhymes. To practise our writing we were given cards upon which these rhymes were printed and we had to copy them into our books. One unforgettable day, I was copying out the rhyme 'I had a Little Pony'. Unfortunately, when I came to the line 'and it was dapple-grey', I ran out of space and tried to squash the words in. When this didn't work, I attempted to rub out that last word with my finger (did I moisten it with a surreptitious lick?). That was an unforgivable sin and I was punished with a few raps of the ruler on my leg. I'm sure I would have cried at this injustice, for I was never punished in this way at home. And anyway, I'd always thought that only the naughty boys were thus treated.

Another mystery of life presented itself when we had to have our medical examinations in the infants' school. I'm sure that the visiting doctor was no ogre, but I suppose that we were all a little afraid. Why was it then, that the child who screamed her loud protestations received special treatment? She got sweets for her outburst; the rest of us got nothing. An early lesson in life? Those who make the most fuss get the best treatment!

A lovely memory that I have concerns the celebration of each child's birthday. Birthday children would stand by Miss Hey, the head teacher, to show their cards and presents (if any). To round off the proceedings, she would produce her cache of bright new pennies, lovingly kept in a soft chamois cloth and the birthday child would take one. To this day, I still have an aversion to parting with any shiny coins I might have in my purse.

On very rare occasions, we would take our little chairs outside, to sit in the grounds of the churchyard for the afternoon story. As adults, we tend to think that those summers of long ago were always filled with hot sunny days. We didn't do this often so perhaps this is a fallacy.

My transfer to the junior school, just a few yards along the road, must have been uneventful, as I recall nothing of that milestone. A bigger school of course, but the same children in the classroom. The sexes were mixed within the classroom, but outdoors we were segregated, both for games lessons and for playtime.

One of the teachers, Miss Garside, seemed quite ancient to us, but most likely she was the same age as our mothers. Perhaps it was because her hair was coiled at each side in 'earphones'. To help us come to terms with unusual spellings and pronunciations, she confessed to us that as a child she would read the word picturesque as 'pictures-cue'. (Even so, I didn't let on that I was a long time in discovering that opticians were not 'opticans'!) We were all full of sympathy for her when we heard that a naughty girl in the class had stuck her pencil into the teacher's arm. We never did find out if the rumours were true, but Miss Garside certainly had red eyes after playtime and the girl in question was missing from the class for the rest of the day.

Our headmaster in the junior school was small in stature, rather like Captain Mainwaring from *Dad's Army*. To this day, I can still picture Mr Gill strutting around the classroom, arms a-flapping, as he sang 'From out of a Wood a Cuckoo Flew'. Mr Gill didn't believe in sending out termly reports or even setting exams. In his opinion, they were a source of concern and only caused trouble amongst parents. Consequently, my first, and only, exams there were for the eleven-plus (elementary exams, I believe they were called then). Sitting these three exams was no ordeal for me. Indeed, the only hardship I had to endure was having to remain silent, but I soon got over that. I thought it quite a novelty – we were issued with brand new golden pencils, printed with the logo 'Boots for the Balms Fund'. I believe that Mr Gill was a patron of this charity.

Attempting to introduce a little culture into our lives one day, Mr Gill asked the class if they knew the name of a famous singer. Greta's hand shot up as she proudly proclaimed 'Deanna Durbin'. Alas, that was not the response that he had hoped for. He went on to extol the virtues of Isobel Baillie, of whom we knew nothing. Greta was right, of course: Deanna Durbin was a lovely singer on the silver screen. Most of us were avid cinema-goers, greatly influenced by what we saw and heard there.

Usually, the teachers did not acknowledge modern-day influences of the music and film world. Our lessons were mainly concerned with the three Rs, occasionally supplemented by history programmes on the radio. I loved listening to the variety of voices in these programmes, and particularly loved the beautiful, lyrical voice of the narrator. It was amusing to witness the speed with which the teacher would dash to the radio to switch it off at the end of the broadcast, before our tender ears could be assailed with unsuitable material.

There was, however, one teacher who was most unconventional, and we loved him for it. The looks of the tall, dark Mr Halstead always reminded me of Humphrey Bogart, another of my screen favourites. He would think nothing of throwing a heavy iron bar to the floor, 'just to wake you up', he would say. Sometimes, he would decide to give us a first-aid lesson, demonstrating the art of bandaging upon an unsuspecting victim (usually a boy, often the same one). One day, as Christmas was approaching, we were practising singing carols, accompanied by Mr Halstead at the piano. Then, quite unexpectedly, he began to play 'I'm Dreaming of a White Christmas'. We couldn't believe our ears and so remained mute until he barked out the order, 'Sing'. And, oh boy, did we sing – with much gusto. At last, an acknowledgement of the outside world with a song that we loved.

From time to time we had student teachers and we did different (gimmicky?) things. On one occasion, we even had a Saturday morning school, where we eagerly went to play with the sweet shop that we had made. I was besotted with Miss Cowan, who taught us for a short time. When she let it be known that it was her birthday, I couldn't wait to rush home and find a present for her. At home, I found a brightly-coloured floral handkerchief (new, I hope), which I sprinkled liberally with perfume. I've often wondered what she thought of my strange offering.

School dinners in the forties were a far cry from today's appetizing multiple-choice menus. Our meals were not cooked on the premises: school dinners for us meant a trek from Church Street, down to Chapel Street and on to Wakefield Road. Thence to 'The Rookery', where we were housed in a long hut (was it a Nissen hut?), to eat our uninspiring meal dished up from huge containers.

It is difficult to imagine the days of rationing now. Dark-coloured bread was

With the church in the background, my brother and a few classmates pose for a patriotic picture on Empire Day. Apparently, the school's costume wardrobe was far from extensive. From left to right, back row: -?- (in a sailor outfit), Beryl Radley as Britannia, Frank Lister. Front row: Stanley Kilvington (my brother), Celia Lipton.

foisted upon us (not the brown bread of today); margarine instead of butter; dried eggs in those ugly grey tins. Our mothers were encouraged to make-do-and-mend and the Dig For Victory signs were everywhere. The shop opposite the junior school supplied us with ha'penny ice blocks. Though only two inches of frozen coloured water, with no stick, they were most welcome. We also bought ha'penny carrots from this shop. We must have been affluent, for we always had another coin with which to scrape off the skin of our carrot. Oranges were not available to us – only to very young children and

expectant mothers, I believe. So it was with horror that I once spotted half an orange lying discarded in the gutter in Brook Street. If it had been mine, I would not have wasted it.

On summer days we would wander down to Frith's on Wakefield Road. There, we would buy potato foam – a substitute for ice cream. We all loved it – what did it matter if it was not real ice cream? To us, the wartime children, it was very welcome on a hot summer's day. We had learned to live without many of the commonplace commodities that had now become unobtainable, forbidden fruits. (In truth, most of us would have had only a dim recollection of ice cream.)

It is said that memories associated with the sense of smell are often the most vivid. Certainly, for me, the smell of rubber evokes vivid memories of our gas mask days. We could never envisage a future life without them; we took them with us, wherever we went. At school, we had regular practice in putting them on. I know that I could still do it properly after all these years: thumbs hooked through the straps, chin in first, then pull the straps to the back of the head to complete the task. Luckily, we were never called upon to put our gas masks to the real test. But we were certainly well trained in the procedure.

We were too young to fully understand the horror of war. It was too remote. We did not feel at risk, and we were not frightened. Only the novelty of new and interesting experiences touched our lives – putting on siren-suits, descending into our Anderson shelters during the night, when the siren sounded.

One such novelty was the practice of assigning us to billets. Every child in the

In the field behind Cross Green Road, celebrating the end of the war. Westfield Cotton Mill is in the background.

school had a nearby house in which to seek refuge should an air raid take place during school hours. It never did. But that did not prevent us making frequent social calls upon our hostess-cum-guardian. Being a very shy child, I doubt that I would ever have made contact with the lady at my billet beyond the initial introductory visit. However, my friend, Dorothy, who was assigned to the same billet, was a much more adventurous girl, and it was at her behest that I made regular calls on our new friend. Whether we were welcomed or merely tolerated, I know not. Either she liked children very

much, or we were too insensitive to realize what little pests we really were.

The nearest we got to the war with the Germans was via our weekly comics. Our own war – the real one – was much closer to home. We took our lives into our hands at home time, whenever we opted to make our journey to Wakefield Road via the enemy camp. Nerves of steel were required to traverse the playground of the dreaded Moldgreen Council School – not a short cut, merely bravado. The children there would jeer at us, calling out 'Churchie Bulldogs'. I suppose we hurled a rejoinder at them, but I do not recall

The horse and cart delivering Comins & Sons' Ice Cream.

remember with affection those bygone days at Moldgreen Church of England School in the war years. Such a happy little school that made so many lasting impressions on us.

Elsie M. Eva

Comins & Son Ice Cream

Both my dad and granddad were called Laurie Comins, and as Comins & Son their work in the 1940s and '50s was manufacturing and selling their own ice cream on a regular ice cream round in Meltham, Marsden, Slaithwaite, Linthwaite and Netherton. My earliest memories are of the splendid horse and cart with the Union Jack flying on the harness collar and our lovely bay horse handsomely turned out with his mane plaited and brasses shining. But times move on and how proud Comins Diploma Ices were when they began delivering in brand new motor delivery vans! Attention to detail was never overlooked and the new vans proudly sported the Union Jack above their windscreens.

The ice cream was always made on Thursday or Friday ready for the weekend round – it was very exciting having an ice cream factory on my doorstep – we called it the dairy. If my brother or sister or I were lucky enough to be around on 'the day' we could look forward to the first lick of the freshly churned, creamy dairy ice cream – it was beautiful, the taste was heavenly. The process used the purest of dairy ingredients; fresh butter and milk were blended and the result, a huge milkshake of creamy white delicious liquid was rolled down into a

our words of retaliation. My sole intention was to reach my goal – the gate to freedom and The Avenue, without sustaining the injury that I always feared was imminent.

I wonder now, where are all the 'Churchie Bulldogs'? The lads with their 'flying helmets'; the lads with the ragged trousers, who swore at the headmaster when they were punished with three strokes of the cane; the lads in the clogs that sent the sparks a-flying as they raced around the playground. The girls that I did hand-stands with against the wall and those that I played 'tag' with around those awful outside lavatories with their leaf-strewn floors. I wonder if they, too,

But times move on. How proud Comins Diploma Ices were when they began delivering in brand new motor delivery vans!

stainless steel cooling pan. We loved to watch it.

The churning and freezing process seemed to take forever, but as a nine year old, with eyes wide open to the back, I was transfixed by the hypnotic turning and folding. Each long deep ice cream container was put into a large brine vat ready for the completion of the freezing/churning process. The stainless steel containers gleamed, just like mirrors. When it was finally finished, to perfection of course, Dad and Granddad took pride in filling all the containers with brand new vanilla ice cream ready for their rounds over the next three days.

I would sometimes go on the round and I can clearly recall the peal of the bronze hand bell that was rung to alert the customers. Out of their houses and gardens they scurried, a regular flow of adults, children, grandmas, granddads, big brothers and sisters with little brothers and sisters coming to the ice cream van. My Dad knew all their names, and always knew how much they had to spend and if it was a cornet, wafer or a dish to fill. 'Thank you, Mr Comins,' came the reply. The raspberry vinegar, which was poured into a little hole in the top of the ice cream cornet, was a special treat and even the grown-ups could rarely resist a squirt. It had no additives, and its tart sweetness was a delicious contrast to the creamy ice cream.

Granddad did another round in his van, different local areas and housing estates. As he got older a younger man was hired to do the weekend work on the ice cream run, but Granddad was always around the dairy to see to it that all the ingredients were right. He certainly made sure that he was still in charge of all the important things! As the years went by popularity grew and the number of ice cream vans expanded into a small fleet, with four of them plying the trade throughout the hills and dales of Meltham and the surrounding area.

In the summertime carnival season the 'Village Queen' galas arrived in Meltham; they always ended up in the village 'rec' (recreation ground). There you would find the hot dog stands, fairground games – hook-a-duck, hoop-la – and, of course, Comins Ice Cream vans were parked up amidst all that was going on. The whole day provided such a lovely spectacle with a happy exciting time had by all.

For obvious reasons wintertime brought a lull in the ice cream trade. Dark evenings brought with them the hard graft – coal deliveries and rearing pigs for sale. As I write this I am amazed by my recollections of the wide range of seasonal work that self-employed 'bread-winners' had to undertake to support the family. For the whole of my early childhood Dad and Granddad both easily moved from summer to winter jobs with ease. Up at the crack of dawn, back home after dark.

It was undeniably a hard slog but definitely worth it. I am left with no doubt that the ice cream business was their pride and joy. I would love to be able to let my children and my siblings' children experience just one of the ice cream making weekends and of course taste that one-minute-old ice cream.

Jacqueline Hardcastle

A Wartime Childhood in Almondbury

I was playing in the garden with an old gramophone record which was an imagined steering wheel. My three-month-old brother Michael was out in his pram, my father was gardening. Mother came out of the house and said, 'Come in, Ernest: I think you'd better listen to this.' We were told: 'Now these are your gas masks. David, yours is like Mickey Mouse, and Michael fits inside his and the air comes through this pump. We have these which fit us. They are kept in these cardboard boxes for carrying. Your identity discs are worn around your neck on string and are in case you become lost. We will use the earplugs if we are bombed.'

An Anderson air-raid shelter was provided which Dad half buried at the top of the garden, covering the top with the dug-out soil on which we made a rockery and planted with flowers. Practice was arranged with a stirrup pump, the children of course being more interested in squirting each other. A sand bag was placed at the top of the stairs, for use against incendiary bombs, and the bath was kept half full of water (we could never removed the brown stain it left). My parents took an interest in English popular songs and taught some to me. Blackout frames were made for the windows and all was checked by the air-raid warden. We had a small bottle of brandy 'for emergencies'. The street lights were extinguished and large tanks of water were placed about the town.

A meeting was held at Tunnacliffe's mill and I walked down, with my mother pushing the pram. A de-activated German incendiary bomb was passed around from family to family so they were familiar with it. It did not look very big. Salvage drives were held for waste paper and scrap metal. Most ornamental railings were removed. 'Pig bins' were put in the street for waste food and also 'bone bins' (for glue manufacture). 'Dig for Victory' and 'Is Your Journey Really Necessary?' posters were put up. A boy evacuee from London came to live across the road.

My father was employed in the mechanics shop at ICI, working shifts of 6 a.m. to 2 p.m. and 2 p.m. to 10 p.m. with an occasional night shift. He joined the factory Home Guard, and once brought his rifle home. It was a very old one. I worked the bolt back and forwards, and looked along the sights. Later he was given a Sten gun and told us that they had been practising demolition. Quite often he had to walk home from work, once arriving home with frost on his overcoat.

'Get up, David, and put your siren suit on. The siren is sounding; there is an air raid!' We went up the back garden, using a shaded torch and carrying our bag of essential documents. Mother said that a lighted cigarette could be seen from the air. We looked to see if our neighbours were out and they were. In the shelter Michael and I were put on the bunk and told to go back to sleep. A loud bang occurred some way off. Father said, 'Someone is getting it.' A discussion then took place about gas masks and it was decided that we would not put them on yet, but await developments. The bangs recurred and we realized that the noise was anti-aircraft fire from the nearby gun-site. We found out later that the blast sucked out the windows of houses close to it. I asked if I could look outside and was told not to, but my father put his tin hat on and took a look. Mother said that I should look for shrapnel in the morning .We heard another family singing in their shelter so we did the same.

The noise of aircraft engines approached and because it rose and fell we knew that it was one of theirs. Flares were seen and bombs dropped some distance away. Later we went to see the craters: one off Lumb Lane and an oil bomb dropped in Molly Carr Wood. More raids occurred later, but such was the secrecy that we only heard about their effects by word of mouth. A barrage balloon drifted over after coming loose from its moorings, dragging its cable and damaging a roof in Wormald Street.

Our house backed onto Almondbury cemetery, where a large hole had been dug. Father had something to do with Civil Defence as he checked these in the other local cemeteries. There was the invasion scare, when Churchill said something about 'taking one with you'. Older boys (aged about eight!) went off into the woods and made 'camps' to hide in.

We had two allotments, growing vegetables and soft fruit, and we also kept rabbits and hens for eating and eggs. These were fed from food produced in the allotment and leftovers mixed with 'balancer meal' which we received instead of our egg ration. We preserved eggs and fruit and made our own jam. Altogether we were busy but were as well-fed as possible. Supplementary vitamins were provided by Ministry of Food, cod-liver oil and orange juice and our own rose hip syrup and later, of course, school milk. Food and clothing were rationed, and sweets to 2oz a week. A spiv came round one day and tried to persuade mother to sell her some sugar. She was refused and would not leave when asked. Father got rid of her when he returned from work after morning shift. Food from America such as spam and processed cheese appeared. Clothing was repaired and passed down to smaller children. Knitted garments were unravelled and re-knitted into something else. Footwear was a particular problem, having to be continually repaired. Scrap leather machinery belts and even old bicycle tyres were used for the purpose. Women whose husbands were in the Forces were especially poor and had to be supported by those around them. Double summer time lengthened the evenings.

Before I joined school mother read to us, and taught me to read so I was familiar with books when I started at the Fenay Lane Council School. All except two of the teachers were women and one of the male teachers had come back from retirement. Slates were sometimes used and books and paper were in short supply. Everyone walked to and from school and came home for lunch. At playtime we watched Verey lights being tested at the fireworks factory at Lepton. The school had its own allotment.

One of my uncles was a sailor and was captured when his ship ran aground off Cape Bon. Another was a fireman in London, was later an engineer on torpedo boats in the Channel, and was posted to Australia before finally returning to England to rejoin the fire brigade. One aunt married a soldier who later died in an accident. Another aunt joined the Women's Land Army at the age of sixteen. She had a leg broken when walking back from a dance with friends, because a car ran them down in the blackout. Later she joined the Wrens, as did her sister. An uncle serving in the Far East, a miner, was sent home to train the Bevan Boys.

A Wellington bomber crashed at Roydhouse, just below Farnley Line, partially demolishing a cottage whose inhabitants were out at the time. An American B17 crashed on the moors above Meltham.

Toys were all second hand except those that were handmade. I was lucky to have a tricycle and later a small bicycle. Our uncles made us wooden models of a Spitfire and tanks. Children's books had a wartime flavour, one being about barrage balloons. As a treat we had indoor fireworks. Holidays were mainly of the 'at home' type in Greenhead Park; we held picnics and paddled in the streams on the moors above Marsden but we did manage to get away once, to Rhyl, I think.

In the Clergy House on Cemetery Road lived the Spanish boys who were refugees from the earlier Spanish Civil War. At a camp on Stirley Hill were the Italian prisoners, some of whom did not go home at the war's end. They wore brown uniforms with coloured patches.

Camouflage nets were made in a barn at the back of Prospect House, anyone with time to spare helped. We were taken on a ramble over the moors above Holmfirth. With plenty of space between them were dumps of bombs. There were very many of them.

One day we were playing cricket in the street (one rule was three gardens and you are out). We heard aeroplanes and counted 142 twin-engine bombers (ours) flying overhead. One night a flying bomb came over. It made so much noise that everyone in the town said that it had flown over their house. I slept through it. Later on, we went on 'half blackout': the gas street lamps were lit and blackout curtains removed. We played out some evenings using torches.

Occasionally we went to the cinema. During the news the liberation of the Belsen concentration camp was shown. The piles of bodies of dead slave labourers were piled 6ft high. The anti-German feeling became stronger. The uncle who was taken prisoner returned home, rather worse for the experience.

We knew victory was coming so we raided the local woods to make a bonfire. Carefully saved fireworks were set off. Bangers were tested by placing them under an empty two-pound treacle tin and timing it until it returned to earth. We also made our own fireworks colouring them with iron and copper filings. Ours did not explode. Those who had them fired Verey lights and let off military thunder flashes. A parade and street party was held. I was taken out to tea and told that as a treat we were having boiled ham. One of my friends obtained a banana, it was skinned and dried and looked rather revolting. Children came from all over to see it. Multicoloured wire became available which was made into jewellery. A rather revolting kind of ice-cream became available.

After the war there was a shortage of accommodation and coal. Food rationing continued. People lived in wash houses, old Army huts on the gun-site and in derelict property in the village which had been condemned years before. Prefab houses were built opposite the gun-site, and later the Fernside Estate. The coal shortage caused back boilers to freeze and fires could not be re-lit because of the danger of explosion so some people were without both heating and hot water. Ice formed on the inside of bedroom windows. We went collecting brushwood from the trees felled in the local woods on our sledges and lorry carts. Local factories closed temporarily. There was bread rationing for the first time (very much later I learned that the grain harvest had failed). It was possible to sledge from the top of Fernside Avenue to Waterloo Rise. After five years of neglect the roads were repaired using tar from the gasworks and pink gravel.

This contained blown up clock mechanisms and the occasional live bullet. Gliders were parked at Fenay Bridge, being quickly robbed of their Perspex windows which were bent into ornaments.

The evacuees returned home, after living here for several years. We poured the brandy on the first Christmas pudding that we ate after the war ended. Michael and I were joined by a sister, Mary.

David Aldridge

The Fish Market Dam

In 1944 in the centre of Huddersfield was a large fish market. Well, it seemed large to me at the time, as I was only ten years old. On our dinner breaks from Beaumont Street School, a bunch of us lads would go to a piece of waste ground at the side of the fish market where there was a dam. As I recollect it was about 10 yards wide by about 15 yards long and of an unknown depth. We would collect doors and planks of wood from bombed or derelict buildings and knock together makeshift rafts and float across the dam on them.

During a school holiday I was lumbered with dragging my six-year-old sister, Beryl, about with me while Mum was out at work. I took Beryl to the fish market dam where she watched as I made this old door into a raft. I tried it myself first and I floated on it fine. Coming into the side Beryl stepped gingerly onto the raft and I pushed off and away we floated. However, all was not well.

What took place next was a similar action to that of a saucer being dropped into a bowl of washing up water, where it slides from side to side dropping deeper into the water

Colin Middleton as a child.

Andrew's Road. Mum was not in. We both expected a good hiding for what we had done and took our clothes off, hung our soggy, smelly, still dripping wet things on the clothes horse in the kitchen and went up to bed to await out fate. Beryl was alright, it was usually me who got the hidings. We laid there listening fearfully for the sound of the door opening and Mum's return.

Eventually the moment arrived and we heard the dreaded sound of the door and then a pause before Mum called out our names. I answered in a weak little voice and in a flash Mum was there. Surprisingly for us she listened to what had happened and then just gave us both a cuddle. Other than a severe warning never to visit the fish market dam again there was no further punishment. My sailing days were of course over then. As we both got older we realized the seriousness of the near double fatality and the reason for our mother's unexpected reaction.

Colin Middleton

each time. The raft started to sink, sliding in toward the centre of the dam our ankles and feet getting wet. Then it changed direction and slid toward the bank, now up to our knees. Neither of us could swim and it was at this point that I grabbed Beryl and threw her with all my ten year old strength toward the bank. My effort in throwing her caused the raft to sink altogether and I was left floundering in the cold smelly water. Six year old Beryl had miraculously been able to reach the bank and struggle out of the water. With a presence of mind far beyond her years she laid down and stretched out, managing to grab my hair and pull me closer to the bank from where I too was able to scramble out of the water.

With stinking, smelly water dripping from our clothes we trudged, with people staring, back to our home in Thistle Street, off St

Annie's Story

I first met Annie Swallow when she was in her late seventies and living in a bed-sitting room in a mansion in Edgerton converted into apartments. Over the years she told me tales of her life that I thought were worth recording so through the winter afternoons of 1988-1989 she reminisced and I wrote down what she said.

I was born on 17 November 1893 at Water Row, New Mill, near Huddersfield. I was one of twins and named Annie, but though my twin, Amy, seemed the stronger of us at birth, she died at three years old. My mother's maiden name was Elizabeth

Sycamore Inn, Holmfirth Road, 1905.

Marshall Mellor (but known as Lizzie) and she married my father, Herbert Swallow, in 1833, both of Holmfirth. I had an older sister, Dora, who was three years eight months older than me.

I was not a strong child and gave my father and mother a good deal of worry about my health. My mother dosed me throughout childhood with cod-liver oil (which I hated) and ipecacuanha wine for bronchitis from which I suffered every winter. Doctors could not be asked to attend patients by telephone in those days; a note had to be taken on foot to their surgeries. The doctor in New Mill went on his rounds on horseback around the villages.

I started school aged five at New Mill National School. Once I heard a boy telling the teacher that his family were moving and I went home and told Mother, who immediately made enquiries and she got the house at Sycamore. She moved the family so often that an uncle said we should have a house on wheels.

The Sycamore Inn on Holmfirth Road was kept by John Smith. Customers who came on horseback tied their horses to the wall. The landlord of the property was Mr Charles Lockwood who lived at The Royds down the road.

After our removal to Sycamore I went to Wooldale School where at first I did not make much progress until one day the vicar, of New Mill, Mr Turnbull, discovered I could read what was on the blackboard quite easily when I was nearer to it. He then realized I had short sight and sent me home with a message for my mother advising her that I go to a specialist. He made an appointment with a consultant up New North Road, who prescribed particularly thick-lensed glasses. At school I was stared at because no other child wore glasses, but it made me better able to read and write. I was a good reader and was often asked to read aloud to the class.

One of the games we played in the school playground was called 'Tut' which is the same as hopscotch.

I went to church and Sunday school at New Mill and on Whit Mondays we girls dressed all in white, and we all paraded round the village singing hymns preceded by our Sunday school banner. We went back to the hall for tea and afterwards ran races in a field on Butterley Lane until dusk fell when we went home so tired we fell straight into bed.

When I were thirteen I flew down that road feeling let loose from school. Nellie Finder and me were thirteen close together. She said they were wanting doffers at Rock Mills, Brockholes. She said to me, 'Shall we go and see if they'll take us on?' So we went the following Monday and were taken on, on short time but I didn't like the work and only stayed a fortnight. I had seen that they required an apprentice at Wooldale Co-op, where they made dresses and coats, and I applied and was taken on.

I was trained by Miss Briggs, who cut out the material. I was 'muggins' as you might say. I was learning my trade and sweeping and dusting and serving in the drapery deptartment as well, selling mantles and ready-mades. We used to measure customers and make their coats and dresses and children's clothes as well. We worked from 8 a.m. to 7.30 p.m. through the week, with half a day off during the week, but until 8 p.m. on Fridays and 6 p.m. on Saturdays. The Co-op was only ten minutes' walk away from home. I had been nervous of giving notice at Rock Mills but my father said, 'Never mind, Annie, I'll do it for you.' I had to walk much further to the mill, and it was January with bad weather.

My father was a joiner on the railway; he went to work early in the morning before we got up. He left our house door unlocked and we found out that a relation living near took advantage of the fact that he had got a good fire going in our kitchen before he went to work, and she came with her shovel and got herself a shovel full of glowing coals to take to her own grate to get it going quickly. Also a crafty hound dog took advantage of the open door and crept down the cellar and stole my mother's Sunday joint.

At the Co-op, we had one hour for a snack mid-day and half an hour every day for tea. We had an 'Onward' oven in which we could warm things, a gas-ring for boiling a kettle and a geyser for hot water. I was able to go home for dinner. It was often after eight o'clock when I got home if there was urgent work to finish, so I had little time for joining my friends at village dances and other events. I did once ask for leave to go early to go to a dance but it caused such a commotion I never asked again.

My father came in one night and said, 'They say there's a fire at t'Co-op.' I arrived for work next morning to find that the grocery department had been burnt out and we were all transferred to a corrugated-iron shop at New Mill while re-building went on. We went back to Wooldale months after the fire.

When I got older, for more experience I

worked at tailors in Huddersfield – Wrigley & Tinker in Alfred Street and Firth & Carr in St John's Road. During the Great War I worked at the Scotch Wool Shop next door to Bradley's the bakers in New Street. I remember one day our doctor, Dr Trotter from Holmfirth, came into the shop to buy some woollen gloves for his little girl and he was so surprised to find me serving him, he said, 'Why, Annie, I had no idea you worked here.' My manageress entertained Australian soldiers in the back room of the shop. One morning she came to work in her usual working clothes but she went behind the scenes and came out wearing a white dress. She left me instructions, 'If the Area Manager comes, Annie, tell him I've just gone round the corner,' and she left me in charge. She came back in half an hour wearing a wedding ring – she had 'gone round the corner' to the Registry Office and married one of the Australian soldiers!

I also worked for a tailor in Shepley, Ernest Hey. He went out measuring and getting orders until he fell off the station platform one day and broke a leg and could no longer work. I was offered a job by Mr Roebuck – 'If you can make a pair of trousers for Mr Hey, you are good enough for me,' he said, but I didn't want to go back to Shepley. I then got a job at New Mill Co-op.

My sister, Nellie, had started work straight from school at Wildspur Mills, New Mill. It was not a woollen mill but spun DMC mercerized yarn. The firm was Copley, Marshall & Co. and she was a hank winder. During the war she lodged with our auntie, and so did I when I was at New Mill, and we went home Saturday to Monday morning. Nellie died at the age of thirty-six from bronchitis.

At New Mill I took stock soon after taking over from the previous manageress. I opened a hatbox which contained fancy summer straw hats and found many of them had been nibbled round the brims. I lifted them out and they fell to pieces and in the bottom of the box were lots of date stones. I called the Grocery Manager, Herbert Fisher, to come and look. When he saw the date stones he said, 'Ee, I allus knew that woman were a mucky beggar!' and he called his young errand boy to clean out the boxes, burn the hats and set mousetraps.

I went to Meltham Co-op in 1919 for 'a bit more' and doing more senior work. I thought when I went to Meltham it were a right funny spot but gradually I got to like it. By this time the family had moved to Thongsbridge and to get to Meltham I had to get a train to Lockwood and change for Meltham and the reverse coming back. My father said, 'You've ridden t'train to death, Annie,' but it was the only way of getting to work. I had to catch the 7.20 p.m. train and it were nearer eight o'clock nor owt before I got home.

Our next move was to Burberry Road, Lockwood. We were known in the surrounding villages as 't'family whose furniture is nivver off of t'flitting cart!' During this removal my mother insisted on personally carrying her most prized possession from Thongsbridge to Lockwood. It was a fragile glass sailing ship with sailor boys in blue climbing up the rigging, under a glass dome. She got it as far as Thongsbridge station booking office and to her horror it somehow slid from her grasp, fell on the floor and lay in hundreds of splinters at her feet. She had to pay a station boy to sweep it up and lamented her loss forever afterwards.

From Lockwood it was easier for me to reach Meltham but I still suffered from bronchitis every winter and it was not

Anne Swallow and Nellie Haigh in the early 1930s.

Miss Imeson, the housekeeper at Meltham Hall, I went with her to stay with her sister at Whitley Bay, and I loved that. I went to the Isle of Wight with some friends but I was not allowed two Saturdays off from work. I had to leave after work on Saturday night, get to London where I stayed one night and got to Shanklin next day.

In the 1950s I went with some friends by coach to Switzerland. On our return, driving through Kent, I looked through the coach window and said, 'Switzerland were all right but I shan't want to go again – England's good enough for me.' We tried Morecambe and Southport but Cleveleys and Blackpool were always my favourites. We enjoyed watching the Pierrots performing on a wooden stage outdoors.

From Lockwood we had another move to Fartown where first Mother died and then Father six months later. He was persuaded to go to the doctor but he would not stop working and even when he was retired he had to go out and help workmen putting pipes in the road. When I was left alone I took in a lodger, first one and then another, but they proved to be a great nuisance. The first one, Mattie, had religious mania or summat, the other burnt a hole through my living-room carpet when I was away, she said she'd left the iron on it when someone came to the door – she never gave me a penny in compensation.

In 1941 I was told of a house to rent in Meltham. I went to see it but turned it down at first until the air raid sirens went one night and I decided I should be safer living in the country, and also the journey from Fartown and back by bus and train was getting too tiring. I was able to take the house so I moved in and stayed nine years.

In 1948 a friend suggested I should retire because of chronic bronchitis which I

helped by the waiting around for trains and buses in all weathers. There weren't many holidays in them days – I only earned 2s 6d a week for two years when I started at Wooldale. We all once went for a week to Blackpool and a friend of mothers asked us out to Cleveleys for tea and we very nearly missed the last tram back to Blackpool. The landlady was just going up to bed with a candle when she let us in. She said, 'I thought you were all in bed!'

We had some cousins in Liverpool who asked us to stay for a day or two and I always remember – the boys took me and Nellie to see a film for the first time and it was a great thrill.

Later on, after I became friendly with

suffered every winter. The idea shocked me at first – 'How could I?' I thought, 'I should have nothing to live on' – but after careful thought I came to the conclusion that it was good advice, and I should be able to live simply until I was eligible for a pension (I was then fifty-four). I began to make plans.

I knew a man who had converted several large old houses into flats and bed-sitters. I rang him and asked if he had a vacant one and soon he let me know he had one at Sedgefield, Edgerton. My friend Nellie Haigh and I went to look at it on my next half-day. We both liked it and I accepted his offer. I had it decorated and Nellie helped me to clean it and I moved in.

I liked living there, though it was a long way from Meltham and all this travelling through the worst winter anybody could remember, in 1947, caused the bronchitis from which I suffered to get worse and my friend said I must retire before the next winter set in. I was frequently absent from work during bronchial attacks and I knew the management didn't like it, so I gave my notice after twenty-six years working at Meltham Co-op.

I did some part-time work to help financially, like serving school dinners, and I lit fires for fellow residents for when they got home from work. When I became sixty and could claim a pension, I stopped working altogether.

One of the front flats was occupied by Miss Ward, a retired English mistress of Longley Hall School. She came to see me in great agitation one winter morning to say that rain was coming through her ceiling and we moved her bed into my room until repairs could be made but she never returned to her own flat. She stayed on with me, paying her expenses for food, electricity and gas and me doing the shopping and cooking for both of us until her last illness when she was taken into St Luke's Hospital.

While she was in hospital I awoke one morning to find smoke everywhere and I turned round and saw flames coming up through the floorboards behind Miss Ward's bed. I ran downstairs looking for a phone and a man came to my rescue. He rang for the fire brigade and when they got there they found my room well alight and only a few items of furniture and other property were saved. By a strange coincidence Miss Ward died at the very same time as the fire happened. The landlord was sent for and he suggested I should move into Miss Ward's flat which I did and after two or three months, Social Services found me accommodation in a bed-sitting room at the Cottage Homes, Waterloo. I went to live there in May 1977 and I have been here ever since. I used to enjoy shopping at Lodge's Supermarket and walking round the district.

I made friends with the other residents, my neighbour being Miss Townend who had been a weaver and long years in a weaving shed had probably caused her terrible deafness. She came to my door one morning in great distress saying she thought she had had a seizure. With great difficulty I helped her back into her room and told the warden, who sent for the doctor, and Miss Townend was taken to St Luke's. The day after that, my leg gave way and I fell myself. I could not attract anybody's attention to help me up until next day and an ambulance was called and I was taken to Huddersfield Royal Infirmary where my leg was found to be fractured. After two weeks I was transferred to St Luke's. I was away nine months altogether, February to November (I think it was 1983). It was decided I should be able to manage if brought back to Cottage Homes if given assistance. Home-helps to make my meals, wheelchair, wheeled trolley, etc.

So I have been on my own ever since. I am now ninety-six years old, sound in mind but not in legs, but it seems I made the right decision to retire early because, though I sometimes suffered bronchitis at Sedgefield, which was cold and unheated on the corridors and stairs, it has bothered me very little here at Cottage Homes where we are centrally-heated and remain snug and warm whatever the weather outside.

This dear, independent old lady died peacefully in St Luke's Hospital, Crosland Moor, on 12 October 1990 within a few weeks of her ninety-seventh birthday.

Audrey Elvin

Wartime Memories of Linthwaite

It was usual practice to go to the morning service, after preliminary Sunday school in the church school, on Sunday morning. We used to go across the road in a long crocodile, up the path through the graveyard to the church. I was always fascinated by a gravestone bearing the inscription 'In loving memory of Catherine Denis, murdered at the Ivy'. The Ivy was a public house down on Manchester Road; I could never imagine how on earth such an event could have occurred there. Our participation in the service was normally very uneventful. We used to sit in the front pews on the left-hand side with little to distract our attention. One Sunday in particular was somewhat different. Father Shaw had just finished his sermon and come down from the pulpit when we were very surprised to see Mrs Shaw approach from the back of the church and whisper in his ear. There was a momentary hesitation, then he stood on the chancel steps to say there had just been a very important announcement on the wireless. Neville Chamberlain had just informed the nation that we were now at war with Germany; it was 3 September 1939. There was an incredible hush in the congregation. Father Shaw then said a special prayer for peace and we all sang the National Anthem. The service finished very shortly and we made our various ways back home, chattering in childish innocence about what had just happened.

Back at home nothing was any different. Mother was busy with our usual Sunday dinner. It was always served at twelve o'clock – Yorkshire pudding with gravy, followed by roast meat and vegetables then pudding – rice, jam roly-poly, spotted dick or something similar – and finally cups of tea. Dad had been busy with his usual Sunday morning jobs. He had always made a practice of listening to the news on the wireless, one o'clock at weekends, six o'clock and nine o'clock during the week. On this particular day it was of even greater importance. We all sat and listened in eerie silence. There were no comments of any kind; it was a very serious atmosphere.

At first life went on in the same old way but gradually changes took place. A week later I should have been going to Royds Hall Grammar School but we received a letter to say school would not start until sometime in October. There was a lot of activity in the household, fastening blackout material to curtains to ensure no light was visible outside. One of our neighbours became an air-raid warden, individuals known as ARP (Air Raid Precautions) wardens. Before long he organized the distribution of gas masks. Adults and older children had the same type, carried in a stout cardboard box, about 6in by 5in by 5in. We each had a gent's white handkerchief and a packet of chewing gum put into our boxes for use in the event of an air raid – chewing gum to calm the nerves, handkerchief for other emergencies. My sister had a triangular bandage in hers. Covers for these boxes became available and they were carried around, slung over our shoulders. Younger children had Mickey Mouse gas masks, coloured red and blue. Babies had entirely different ones which completely enclosed them. We were also given identification cards, each of which had a personal number, e.g. KMLJ/170/6, in which the final number indicated position in the family.

Sometime in October school was opened. We had to carry our outdoor coats and gas masks, as well as schoolbooks, from room to room, wherever we were being taught. Large brick air-raid shelters had been built in the school grounds. Air-raid practices occurred regularly. Children from the lower forms used the school shelters, older children went out into the Anderson shelters installed in the gardens of the houses in Victory Avenue. These were very orderly events. The school bell gave the alarm. We all lined up, complete with coats and gas masks, followed the teacher in charge at the time into our respective shelter accommodation. After a lapse of time those who were in school shelters lined up outside and had roll call. Those outside school were called out by the member of staff and we all made our way back to class.

My sister became involved in another group, which I believe were called Fire Watchers. They used to do overnight duty from time to time in one of the large schools or public buildings. Unless there had been an air-raid warning I think it was usually uneventful. What we had always called the mill buzzers, which had regulated the daily timetable of the mill workers, were used as sirens. The warning was an intermittent wailing sound, the 'all-clear' a constant sound. Air raids were infrequent but usually occurred at night. The warning would go and we would lie in bed, listening for the monotonous drone of enemy aircraft. They made a quite different sound from our own. Sometimes we would peer behind the bedroom curtains, never any lights on, watching the searchlights scouring the sky for the planes. Occasionally we would hear the scream of a bomb being dropped and the subsequent thud, but those were rare events. Sometimes there was anti-aircraft fire. In one raid, early in the war, we could see small fires up the valley in the Slaithwaite area. Dad said they had dropped a 'Molotov Bread Basket', a clutch of incendiary bombs.

It was not long after the outbreak of war that the LDV (Local Defence Volunteers) were formed, later known as the Home Guard. They were a far cry from the buffoonery of the *Dad's Army* series, being mostly men who had seen active service in the 1914-1918 war. Dad joined them. I believe they were under the command of Colonel Charles Lockwood of Black Rock. They used to meet on a regular basis. Polishing brass buttons, black boots and cleaning the rifle became a part of the weekly pattern. They would sometimes appear on church parade, most particularly on Armistice Sunday.

Dad also joined what I think was called the Observer Corps. There was an air of secrecy about these matters, so little was ever said. He used to go regularly on a Saturday to somewhere on the outskirts of

Huddersfield. On rare occasions I went with him. It was a long ride on the trolley bus and then a walk across fields. I always thought it was in the Fixby area, but I have no evidence. The observation post was a wooden hut with radio equipment and binoculars etc. Messages would be passed to and fro and Dad would track any aircraft which appeared in the sky, making notes appropriately. I occupied myself playing in the rural environment.

Ration books were distributed quite early on in the war, along with clothing coupons and sweet coupons. Coupons had to be surrendered with purchases but ration books were marked off every week. We had our groceries from Milnsbridge Co-operative store. A member of staff used to call every Tuesday, collect our order book and mention any special offers available. The order was delivered later in the week and the bill paid on Saturday morning. It was a regular thing to have 6lb of sugar and 2lb of best Danish tub butter every week. I sometimes wonder what on earth happened to all that butter but it was used for baking etc. Margarine never appeared until wartime. Our usual shopping list changed considerably. Danish butter vanished, as did the supplies which came from the outposts of the Empire, as it was then known. We received the allocations of butter, tea, sugar etc. to which the family was entitled each week. If the store was lucky to receive a delivery of tinned fruit, dried fruit, tinned salmon etc. we were always allocated these with our order.

Shopping followed a very different pattern. Mother used to go to town early; I often went too. We always made a bee-line for the market hall. There were certain stalls which we made for. The Caledonian Biscuit Company in the upper market hall was a regular port of call. Often the blinds would be drawn and a small queue would have formed outside, waiting hopefully. Eventually an assistant would appear and get organized for selling, or the expectant customers would be told there was nothing available that day. Each member of the queue would be able to buy a bag of biscuits, usually 1lb. There was no question of choice, whatever was available was gratefully received, sometimes there were only broken biscuits but that did not matter. Sometimes shoppers would pass messages round as they bustled along – Lodge's have tinned fruit, Redman's have tins of salmon – and these shops were visited as quickly as possible. Sometimes supplies ran out before we got to the front of the queue but we always had a go. Sometimes we were able to get dried apple rings or dried bananas. They were not terribly inviting but we made the best of them. Sometimes it was possible to get oranges form Lindon Smith's, the greengrocers on Shambles. Shopping became a quest for anything that would add to our weekly rations.

Meat was also rationed. Our butcher was George Dixon, a farmer at Blackmoorfoot. He used to come with his horse-drawn van every Friday evening. There was always a discussion about what was available. Sometimes we were lucky and able to have an ox tail. This was not included in the ration so we enjoyed oxtail stew with dumplings from time to time. We had a lot of home deliveries. Willie Taylor, whose family had the fish & chip/fish/poultry/vegetable business at the top of Morley Lane, used to deliver fish every Tuesday and Thursday. Sometimes he would arrive with a parcel of fents or samples of worsted material. These were ideal for making skirts etc. We were grateful to have them, no questions were asked. Bread was also delivered by the Co-op bakery van. White bread disappeared. Flour was less refined and we had what was termed the national loaf, somewhat off-white in colour. There was also a greengrocer with a pony and flat cart. He was always called the Apple-ripe man. I think this was because of his calls as he arrived. The Roberts family from Hollin Green Farm delivered their milk by horse-drawn float. The horse was always beautifully turned out, shiny black leather and polished brasses.

On Saturday at midday we often had fish and chips from the Ivy Fisheries on Manchester Road, run by Frank Taylor and his wife, Ivy. Occasionally we would have fishcakes; these were two large slices of potato with a large fillet of fish in between, fried like the fish. Fish and chips cost 6d, fishcakes were 2d extra, specially cooked. During the week we sometimes had fish and chips at suppertime from Mrs Tyson, just down the road, opposite the Folly. She also sold bread, biscuits, tinned goods and sweets. At times she had a notice on the door 'Not cooking tonight, no fish'. Considering what was happening in the North Sea and the Atlantic it is astonishing that we had the quantity and variety of fish at that time.

Life at school continued with our regular air-raid practices. We became involved in the Ship Adoption Society. Our ship was a Danish vessel under the command of Capt. Hans Pedersen. It had presumably escaped the occupation and was working alongside the Royal Navy. We used to knit scarves and socks for the crew and rustle up gifts of toiletries etc. I think there must have been a special allocation of wool as it was in quite short supply and only available on coupons. Capt. Pedersen used to visit school occasionally. There were no Speech Days during the war, probably because of the difficulties of going out after dark – street lighting had virtually disappeared, vehicles had shaded headlamps and buses had their windows blacked out. The only other outstanding thing I remember was making eggless chocolate buns. I only took domestic science for a year. It was not my favourite subject and certainly not enhanced by those buns.

When the bombing of London started evacuees were brought into the area. There were also one or two from the East Coast. Once we had adapted to their accents and they'd become accustomed to ours they were rapidly absorbed into the community. Some of them were so comfortable they never went back.

Listening to the news on the wireless was an essential part of our lives. On Sunday, before the nine o'clock news, all the national anthems of the Allies were played. I always found that a very moving experience. When the long awaited day of victory arrived I remember being in St George's Square. It was absolutely packed with happy people. It would be impossible to describe the emotions displayed. Each and every one of us had a wealth of different experiences, many tinged with sadness. However, there was a tremendous feeling of optimism. We were about to make a fresh start.

Margaret A. Town

Life at the Grey Horse

The year 1945 saw one war end and another begin as our family moved into the Grey Horse in Chapel Hill. My dad had been a waiter there and also frequented the pub while on wartime fire-watching duties at Thomas Broadbent's Engineers. The move itself was not uneventful as somehow my dad

Chapel Hill in the 1940s. Note the cobblestones and the lack of cars. (Huddersfield Daily Examiner)

Bert and his spoon-playing pal Arnold Garrety ended up with the job of transporting my cot from our old house in Freehold Street, Primrose Hill to the pub. Unaware that the cot was collapsible they tackled it in true Laurel and Hardy style, carrying it down all the 'cat steps' to the bottom of Whitehead Lane and across the footbridge over the River Colne into Colne Road and up the hill all in one piece!

The Chapel Hill area was very different then: the road was still cobbled, there were lots of houses on Milford Street and Dale Street where houses on one side were under

dwellings beneath the terraced homes along Manchester Road. The textile mills were thriving and at 5.30 in the evening you could not see the pavements for the throng of workers streaming home – just like L.S. Lowry's paintings that became so popular years later.

The Grey Horse was not without competition. There were at least ten pubs between the top of Chapel Hill and Lockwood Bar. In fact a popular pub crawl was to have a drink in each one. But these were the days when few people had TV sets or cars and so went to their 'local' for a drink, perhaps after queuing at the Grand cinema on Manchester Road to watch such stars as Betty Hutton, Anna Neagle and Clarke Gable.

I mentioned another war starting because, although the Grey Horse was a lively, friendly, busy place, it also got a bit wild, especially at weekends. My dad employed three waiters, more if the 'Buffs' had a meeting upstairs. He also hired a pianist named Herman who sported a black beret. I loved the smell and atmosphere of the place at opening time, all mopped and polished, clean sawdust in the spittoons (often my job) and that lovely scent of fresh beer. I frequently helped to put the bottles on the shelves, Town Majors and Guards Ale etc., supplied by Hammond's brewery at Lockwood.

Saturday night could develop into a scene such as those I observed in the Wild West saloons at the Saturday matinées at the Lounge cinema in Newsome Road. A number of huge labourers would arrive from the Model Lodging House across the road and be drinking happily together. Then one of them would decide Saturday night was not the same without a bit of a barney. I would be playing in the kitchen and hear the sound of breaking glass, followed by a whole lot more along with men shouting and women screaming. Our dog would add to the bedlam as my dad rushed into the kitchen to ring the police, with his white shirt torn and bloodstained (not usually his). Sometimes the waiters, who were a resilient bunch, would have things sorted before the police arrived. One big Welshman who played prop forward for Fartown used to tell my dad 'any trouble and you stay behind the bar – I'll handle it.' He usually did, sometimes assisted by my uncle Pal, a burly ex-miner from Barnsley, who

lived with us at the time after losing his wife in a horrific road accident. I remember watching out of the upstairs window as the battling pair filled Dale Street with a heap of intemperate bodies, all of this to accompaniment of tunes like 'I'll Take You Home Again Kathleen'.

Another of my uncles was the hero one Easter Sunday morning. We had all got up early and dad went down to the cellar to find it ablaze. A painter from the brewery had left a can of flammable liquid next to the coke fired central heating stove. Dad shot back upstairs to telephone the fire brigade. Myself and my cousin Joyce, whose family were staying with us for the holiday weekend, ran out into Chapel Hill to wave and shout directions to the firemen but, to our dismay, they drove straight past thinking my dad had said Shaw and Greenhaigh Ltd and not the Grey Horse. While the brigade were arriving in Albert Street to discover their mistake my Uncle Tom, Joyce's dad, a butcher from Bailey, had put the fire out using the hose dad used to swill the beer cellar.

One sign that the other war had not long finished was when the dustbin men took their break in the pub back yard to play football. Usually there would be one with a patch on his back bearing the letters POW.

My older brother Derek, who later kept a pub in Rastrick for twenty years, almost had a much shorter life. We often played on the canal bank and one day he knelt on the lock, trying to catch a fish with his hands and fell in. His mate Brian saved his life, grabbing him by his hair and getting him safely out of the very deep water. They had their photograph in the *Examiner* and that brave young lad grew up to become a police inspector. Mind you I almost wished Brian had not bothered after some of the scrapes

All dressed up in Greenhead Park, 1940s. Tpny Madocks is at the front left with Michael Smith. From left to right, back row: my brother Derek, sister Barbara, Joan Livesey and Rayner Smith. The Smith brothers lived in the Grey Horse yard and Joan in Chapel Hill.

my dear brother got me into in the years that followed. One day he was standing on the roof of an outside loo in the Grey Horse yard calling me names. I picked up a half-brick and lobbed it at him. He dodged to one side, leaving the missile to go over the wall. It landed smack in the middle of the roof of a neighbour's gleaming Austin 7. To make matters worse he was polishing it at the time!

Another escapade happened one night when the 'Buffs' I mentioned earlier (I think they were the working man's equivalent of freemasons), were having one of their meetings upstairs at the pub. The door to their meeting room had a small sliding opening in it so that when someone knocked the doorman would open this little slot and ask them the password to gain entry.

One night my brother persuaded me it would be a good idea if I tiptoed from our bedroom, knocked on the door and ran back into our room undetected by the doorman. I innocently accepted the challenge only to find the bedroom door locked as I made my hasty retreat. When the doorman slid open the aperture there I was in my pyjamas, dashing about on the landing, desperately looking for somewhere to hide. The phrase 'headless chicken' had not been coined back then but it would have been very apt!

Despite the pub's sparkling cleanliness we were once overrun with cockroaches. This was in the days when chewing tobacco was popular. The less well-off amongst the clientele would keep an eye on the ashtrays for something to chew. One old character, nicknamed 'Tuffy', who lived at the working men's home, grabbed what he thought was a nice piece of 'twist' and it was in his mouth before he realised that it was one of our invading insect friends. That story still makes me shudder fifty years later.

On leaving Stile Common School, where he had excelled in goal despite his lack of height, my brother started work as an apprentice joiner for John Parker & Son, who were based in a hut down a yard in Chapel Hill. He was only 4ft 11in tall and our mum had to turn his overalls up to his knees. She almost had a fit when he worked on a roof in Brockholes on his first day. One of his next jobs was helping to build a garage for the owner of a new café opening just a bit further up the hill from the pub. The proprietor was among the very first Asians to come to Huddersfield. His name was Mohammed Ali but everyone knew him as Ronnie. My brother said Ronnie was getting this enormous car. It turned out to be a two-tone Ford Consul but it seemed very flash in those days of Austin 7s and Jowetts. We sometimes went to the café for pie and peas (very Indian!) on Saturday lunchtimes when Mum was busy in the pub.

Our affluence knew no bounds by 1953 and we got a floor-standing, black and white TV set with a 12in screen in time for the Coronation and the Blackpool *v.* Bolton cup final, remembered as 'the Stanley Matthews final'. We had a kitchen full of

Tony's old house at Freehold Street, Primrose Hill, in the centre of the photograph. (Huddersfield Daily Examiner)

Bert and May Maddocks, former licensees of the Grey Horse, are pictured here in the 1960s, still hard at work as tenants of the Wagon and Horses, Leeds Road.

friends, neighbours and customers for both events. Sadly 1953 was to be our last year at the Grey Horse but the memories have lived on in our family for half a century.

Tony Maddocks

Huddersfield Textiles

My experience of textile mills in Huddersfield started as a school leaver in September 1948. Of course textiles had been a thriving industry in this area long before that, both for woollens and worsteds. There were many textile mills spread around the Huddersfield area, but now only a few remain due partly to man-made fibres.

My first job was as an apprentice mender at William Thomson's down a yard by the canal opposite the bottom of Whitacre Street, Leeds Road, Deighton. Our director was Benjamin Franklin Broadhead, who also had interests in other mills in the Huddersfield area. Thompson's were renowned for some of the finest fancy worsteds in this area, with the name and Huddersfield woven into the edge each side of the roll of cloth.

We worked from 7 a.m. to 5 p.m. with a half-hour lunch break. My starting wage was 37s 6d per week. We started out learning on squares of white twill worsted: a thread would be pulled out and we had to put a red thread back in stitch for stitch, then we progressed to more threads out together and holes. I had only been there a couple of weeks when our Mrs Mender (the teacher), Laura Osterfield of Lockwood, cut a hole eighteen threads each way (weft and warp), I had made such a good job of it Laura showed it to the manager Bert Ellis and I was given 1d an hour increase in pay, more than the other apprentices.

In between learning to mend we had to learn to use sewing machines, to number the pieces in our turns, until a new lot of apprentices came. We then progressed to mending big rolls of cloth from the loom. After the Greasy Percher had examined them for faults, our boss/percher called Henry Mallinson stood in front of the a big window and pulled the cloth over a frame.

It was the menders who found most faults and on this depended how much money we were able to earn; too many faults meant low pay as it was piece work. We worked in pairs, had a long table where the top lifted to a slant and as we pulled the cloth over we had to feel for knots and pull them up into the back (wrong side) with our irons making sure nothing was left tight. We had to mark faults in the yarn – too thick, too thin, twisted too tight, or too loose, then we had to set about mending the greasy cloth as it was at this stage, our tackle being a thimble, pointless needles and scissors.

From the mending loom the rolls of cloth were taken to Longwood Finishing Company for the next process: scouring, finishing, pressing, etc. Some cloth also needed dyeing. The beautifully finished

Marjorie Medrek (front) at the mending table with partner Sheila (née Derbyshire).

Steps leading to canteen and mending room. The skips would hold the bobbins of yarn.

Works Annual Trip: menders and weavers having lunch at Blackpool Pleasure Beach.

cloth was then taken back to Thompson's warehouse where final checks were made and then the cloth was packed and dispatched all over the world. Jack Schofield was the boss there.

I worked at Thomson's for fourteen years; during that time B.F. Broadhead became associated with a Charles Chlore from London who eventually bought Thomson's and others. We were combined with Kaye and Stewart's Albert Street, Lockwood. Nothing was to change, the workforce where told, but eventually when textiles started to decline they closed down, the end of an era.

In the meantime I worked for approximately three years at Ward Pitchers, Lockwood and Vickerman's at the bottom of Crossland Moor. Altogether I had twenty-five years in mending cloth, very tedious but satisfying. We mended hopsack, gaberdine, birds-eye, cavalry twill, checks and other fancy patterns – some with stripes.

Thomson's also had a yarn room, winding room, pattern room (where samples were woven on handlooms), warping and weaving sheds, greasy percher, menders and despatch warehouse.

One good thing about my job was that I was able to work at home when my children were young, and in school holidays or if the kids were ill. I did mending work for Clive and Conrad Thomas Tanyard, Quarmby. Their work was for a Scottish firm, Reid and Taylor – very fancy patterns and a high standard of work required. A suit of their cloth made at Vic Friend's tailor, Wood Street, Huddersfield was very expensive.

When I did eventually go back to the

mill, after three years I was made redundant. Textiles were in decline and I had to turn my hand to other work.

Marjorie Medrek

To Chapel

Hall Bower chapel was a dark dreary place to me, a small child in the 1950s. I was born to a farming family living near Castle Hill, and was sent to chapel each Sunday by my parents, not because they were God-fearing, but so they could take a rest from both the farm and me, having laboured with us both the previous six days.

I wasn't happy at the prospect of a walk over the three fields to get there, with only cows or sheep for company, and perhaps the odd daisy or buttercup nodding its head in the breeze, and always the cowpats (or country pancakes as we called them) covering my path. My tiny fists were clenched tight with my silver thruppenny bit, my offering to the collection, with the sound in my ears of Mum saying. 'Don't lose it, Valerie Jean.' Sometimes I did drop it into a pancake where on I'd stick my fingers in to retrieve it, so as not to look silly in chapel when the plate came round (it seemed logical to a four-year-old).

I sat on the wooden bench, looking round. Everyone and everywhere seemed dark, the paintwork, the Bible, the man at the front who wore a dress. The only men I knew were rough and ready farmers who wore check shirts and patched trousers. I didn't know the man in the

Office cleaners and canteen staff trip to Blackpool. My mother is second from the left.

Valerie Jean aged four at Farnley Rec.

Treadle sewing machine.

For years and years Sundays were like that, the same man, the same hard bench that numbed your bum and that funny smell of moth balls filling the air, a pattern broken only for short holidays in either Brid or Whitby, where we had relations and could usually get away cheaply or for free if my mum helped out in their boarding houses. My father never went on these trips, as animals knew not of humans changing the pattern. Today it seems an unreal existence – no fear, no violence, no strangers. I knew everyone or rather they knew me, or certainly my family.

We shopped from Co-op carts that

dress, but he was there each week, shouting and stomping about waving his arms wildly. The only time adults shouted in my presence was if I'd been naughty, but this chap shouted every Sunday. I thought him a strange chap who was bad tempered and wore dresses. I never saw him anywhere but there, so I assumed he lived there and invited us all in.

I was always cold sitting on that bench – cold, fed up and hungry. I'd have my breakfast, but the long walk to visit the 'grumpy man' as I called him soon resulted in hunger pangs. I didn't know his name – and he never asked mine – but I often wondered why his frock was always black and what he wore underneath it. I'd no black dresses at all; my Sunday best dress was, complete with matching knickers, usually a home-made affair, run up by my granny on the Singer

Valerie's grandmother, and her only son, John, (Valerie's father), sitting on the front lawn around 1933.

came weekly up the steep hill from Berry Brow, writing our list and counting the divi. Clothes, cottons and what we'd term today as sundries were purchased from a Mr Kaye – a traveller who called monthly to the farm – and kept his goods in huge black suitcases. What we ate was very different too – no frozen meals, in fact we'd no fridge till 1968, having made do for nearly forty years with the meat safe, a grille over it to stop the flies and a concrete slab in the cellar, a custom cover for leftovers on tin plates. We'd no milk bottles; milk stayed in the cow till we needed it, and then we took the tripod stool and bucket to Daisy, Maisie or Queenie and pulled our own.

I had such a shock in 1969 when we upped sticks to live in Moldgreen. I saw people just like me who weren't white, proper shops that had a bell that rang out when the door opened, goods that changed daily. I ate take-out fish and chips for the first time, and we washed our clothes at a place named a washette.

It was too far to travel to Hall Bower so I joined Moldgreen church. What a relief to note the man at the front was much quieter than the chap at Hall Bower and also wore trousers – this I could understand. I knew his name – Leslie – and I knew he didn't live at the church, because we'd been invited to his home, mum and I, where his wife served strong tea and rock buns. Those buns were terrible! I disgraced myself by taking a big bite into one and quietly spitting it out into the hand, everyone looked at me. My mother opened her handbag quickly and put the offending bun into it. The trouble was in the baking. At home my granny did all our baking; in her working life she had been a cook for a Quaker School in Ackworth and she baked to perfection. The vicar's wife was

no match, I'm afraid.

We were never asked again and I was told off by my mother on the walk home. Never again would I accept anything I couldn't eat or didn't like the look of – better to refuse than to offend. (I've never liked rock buns to this day.) That same vicar married me the first time round. I was only eighteen years old and naturally people thought, 'Oh, she's got a bun in the oven,' but I hadn't; in fact I have never been blessed with children at all. I said to my mother, 'The bun's not in the oven but rather in the handbag!' and we'd laugh.

Sadly the church is gone now, standing as it did next to the Regal cinema. All Moldgreen has changed since I lived there. The vicar and his wife are maybe baking in the kitchen in the sky. Hall Bower's still there though – I visited it again this year, my first call in over 30 years. There was no dark paint, no hard benches, no long faces, nor men in frocks – it seemed smaller than I had remembered. I'd gone to a concert; it was Saturday night so I didn't expect to see a vicar, and I was greeted warmly. People were in bright array, mood buoyant, lively music wafted over us – inside I was still remembering people long gone, places so different and yet the same. Hall Bower chapel still stands there still three fields from the farm – still preaching the word of God, perhaps to tiny four-year-olds sent by their parents because it's Sunday.

Valerie Carter

A *Penny Magazine*

A penny magazine, packed from cover to cover with interesting features and

Woodhouse church, Huddersfield.

advertisements – that was Woodhouse church magazine of September 1901. A hundred years on, Woodhouse Vicarage is for sale at £165, 000 and there has been a big decline of churchgoing in the twenty-first century. However, we can still look back to more Godly days in that old magazine, with a glimpse into another way of life....

Under the heading 'Baptised into Jesus Christ during the proceeding month', the first of seven babies' names was Joe Herbert Crawshaw. No wonder that particular magazine remained a treasured memento of the Crawshaw family. How unusual to open a publication today and see that a baby had been christened Joe Herbert. Other births recorded at Woodhouse where an Ethel, two Normans, Frank, another Frank with Edgar for a middle name, Ernest, and John. Marriages showed similar names. On 10 August 1901 the marriage was solemnized between John William Wheeler and Ellen Brooke, and also between William Atkinson and Clara Cook. On the 31st Harry Cheetham and Ellen Littlewood, of Leeds Road were wed. Names typical of the early years of the twentieth century continue in the records of burials, Mary Ann, Oscar, Florence, Alice Maud, Mary, Minnie, Maud.

There was a Bible Class for men at 3 p.m. on Sundays. On alternate Tuesday evenings at 8 p.m. it was the ladies' turn, with another on Wednesday afternoons at 2.45 p.m.

Local tradesmen advertised in their church magazine. John Netherwood, music and instrument dealer, of 81 Sheepridge Road, chose a drawing of a Grecian type lady, all drapes and coiled hair, delicately playing a cello, to announce that lessons were also given in piano, harmonium, organ, singing and theory. Another page showed a sturdy sketch of a bull, bringing readers' attention to the wares of Allan Balmforth, butcher, also of Sheepridge. Pickled tongues and beef were his specialities. A.D. Shaw, General Draper of 94 Deighton Road, advertised plain and fancy dress materials, hardings and

household linen, bed ticks and ticking, flannels, prints and calicoes, shawls, blouses, aprons, ladies' and children's underclothing, ribbons, laces, veilings, beltings, bindings, braids, crochet and knitting cottons, sewing threads, twists, small wares of every description. He also sold oilcloths; the very name 'oilcloth' almost conjures up that almost forgotten pervasive aroma. Mr Shaw ended his advertisement 'Closed Wednesday instead of Tuesday.'

Granddad Taylor's shop in 1901 also closed for a half-day at 1 p.m. on Wednesdays. For any establishment to be open on a Sunday was unheard of. The twenty-first century may have undreamed-of technology, but it has lost

that sense of peace our forefathers enjoyed mid-week and on Sundays – perhaps even more important to the stability of a society.

George Saville, Wholesale and Retail Drapers of 4 and 6 Queen Street, advertised that sewing societies would be charged only wholesale prices.

In 1901 furniture, like marriages, was meant to last a lifetime, maybe with a little help on occasions. Richard C. Taylor, upholsterer of 56 Deighton Road, made it known through Woodhouse church magazine that old furniture could be reupholstered, re-covered, and made equal to new, in Morocco, velvet, tapestries etc. Clogger, boot and shoe repairer John William Battye of 10 Hillhouse Road was 'prepared to take in repairs' at his residence, 11 Sheepridge Road.

In September of 1901 the Woodhouse clergy consisted of Revd A. Whorlow MA, and Revd F.S. Playne BA. The organist and choirmaster was Mr John Netherwood. Other officials listed included teachers at day schools. How teachers were looked up to in those days! They dressed in dignified manner and behaved with decorum, and discipline even in classes of sometimes forty or more was not a problem. They included Mr W. Sharpe, Certified Master, Mrs Sharpe, Certified Mistress, Miss Crawshaw, assistant mistress, and Miss Spencer, assistant mistress.

During August church expenses amounted to £14 11s 4d; the altar fund raised £2 1s 4d, the Men's Gift £1 16s 9d, the Sick and Poor Fund £1 14s 9d, and the Children's Gift £1 5s 6d.

Woodhouse church magazine included a story by a Mrs G.S. Reaney, author of *Our Daughters: Their Lives Here and Hereafter*, also *Daisy Snowflake's Secret* and others. The September story, in similar vein was entitled *Better Than Rubies*.

The heroine's name was Letitia; she was a governess. In the manner of the time, she was given to blushing on encountering a friend (male) of her brother. The heart throb of a hundred years ago was drawn with jet-black hair parted down the middle, a walrus moustache and ankle-length overcoat. He walked with a cane in one hand, tall silk hat raised in the other. The caption reads 'He Was walking with a Friend.' The story is further typified by this sentence, 'Letitia felt uncomfortable. Arthur's manner was so flippant, that for a moment she did not feel proud of him as an acquaintance.' To ensure further sales of Woodhouse church magazine the story was to be continued.

Few today, if any, will recall the Huddersfield Toilet Club, where the business of hair cutting, singeing, shampooing and shaving of gentlemen took place. The Proprietor was S.H. Thwaite of 6 Station Street, entrance via Byram Arcade.

D. Harper, Confectioner of Fartown Bar, created wedding and birthday cakes to order, and was an agent for Cadbury's, Rowntree's and Fry's chocolates. They also catered for funeral teas. So did my granddad, John Taylor, then in business as a grocer and provision merchant. He had an advertisement in the magazine, although he regularly attended Deighton Methodist church. He advertised home made jams and marmalade (made by Grandma and a few lady helpers in the village) and prime home-boiled hams.

They swung from the shop ceiling, as did flycatchers in hot weather. He also was an agent for Welch's grape juice, 'Cobcordials' or Pure Fruit Beverages. A life-long teetotaller, he proudly advertised 'The Great Temperance Beverage', as well as non-alcoholic 'Invalid Port', sold in pint bottles at only 1s 6d.

J.W. Firth, 9 Sheepridge Road, was a milk dealer, grocer, confectioner and sold home-made bread, children's toys, tobacco and cigars, as well as ice-cream made from pure milk. Miss Copley of Byram Street used to be a well-known name in the town. She is advertised in the magazine as 'Ladies' Manicure and Hairdresser, hair dressed in all the latest styles, for Promenade, Evening, and Fancy Dress Balls. Ladies' combings may

be made up in any style at reasonable charges.' Theatrical and other wigs were on hire. In smaller print (to interest only a minority group?) was 'Hair dyed and coloured any shade.' Lessons were given to ladies' maids in the art of hairdressing. Of course, in 1901, hair was long and usually luxuriant, due to brushing a hundred strokes a night and perhaps using Harlene hair tonic.

False eyelashes were not then *à la mode*. Miss Copley sold 'a tonique for the hair which produces luxurious hair and is unequalled for weak and thin eyelashes' at 1s and 2s 6d a bottle. Her hours of business were from 9 a.m. to 7.30 p.m., closing on Wednesdays at 2 p.m. A. Beaumont, hairdresser and tobacconist of 238 Bradford Road Fartown, sold Smoke Bar Mixture, at 4d per ounce or 2oz for $7\frac{1}{2}$ He also re-covered and repaired umbrellas. At the time a gentleman's hairdresser and umbrella maker also traded in Market Place: Mr George North, whose establishment's entrance was in a passage next to Mr A. Morton's Dining Rooms.

Sunderland Bros of Hillhouse repaired and re-set kitchen ranges; hashing machine rollers were put in and old ones returned. Walter Neaverson was already trading as a glass and china merchant opposite the parish church. At the time of writing, happily the name of Neaverson and their beautiful china shop is still gracing the town on Byram Street. What a loss it is when old established firms are no more. Sadly, Wheatley Dyson is no more. In September 1901 Fartown boasted a livery stables. Mr Darwin was a stagecoach proprietor there. There is a sketch of the stables in the magazine.

No magazine worth its name forgot to

Joe Taylor's Yorkshire Village Shop, 1930s.

drive on 21 August to Sunny Vale Gardens. The party included eight probationer choirboys. An item about the cricket club covered the new pavilion opened at Halifax St Mary's, which had been built entirely by voluntary labour in spare time by members of the club and Bible class. An account was given of the choirboys' trip to Bridlington, along with a copy of a letter sent by Lady Carlisle of Castle Howard printed after a choir trip to her home. She wrote 'You have given real pleasure by your singing of that beautiful hymn, *Lead Kindly Light*, and the other music you gave was delightful.' She concluded, 'Guests are ever welcome here, especially when they have music in their souls and sweet voices to give it forth.'

No Huddersfield church magazine would be complete without an advertisement for one of the most popular grocery establishments of former days. Wallace's, 'The People's Grocers', portrays a bewigged footman bowing graciously towards these prices – 'Wallace's Golden Flower tea, 1s 8d, 2s, and 2s 4d per pound. Best Value in the Kingdom.' As was Woodhouse Church Penny Magazine.

Hazel Wheeler

include cookery items! A small corner was given to 'Homely Cookery'. Churchgoers reading the September edition learned how to make suet crust, Suffolk dumplings, and how to dry herbs. (I remember coming home from school on a snowy dinner time to stew and dumplings, HP sauce, and roly-poly jam suet pudding with white sauce – Paradise!)

There was a piece about great church musicians, another about the Indian famine by the Most Revd J.E.C. Welldon DD, Lord Bishop of Calcutta. There was also a moralistic story, *Father of the Fatherless*, a harvest hymn, words and music, a Bible quiz, and a puzzle corner – not forgetting perennial tips on gardening.

Notes about day trips included the 'Working Parties' outing, and a charabanc

Woods fish and poultry shop, 1920s or '30s.

Scholars' Christmas Treat.

COME AND SEE the wonderful

ANIMATED PICTURES

(The Finest ever exhibited),

Including a PANTOMIME

In the

Town Hall, Huddersfield,

ON BOXING DAY, (SATURDAY, Dec. 26th, 1908)

Commencing at 2-30 o'clock. Doors open at 2 p.m.

Admission for Children under **14**, Balcony 6d., Area 3d., Gallery 2d.

Adults—Balcony 1/-, Area 6d., Gallery 3d.

FRESH PICTURES AT NIGHT. and . . . .

. . . . JOHN DRAKE, the Yorkshire Comic.

Commencing 7 p.m., 1/-, 6d. and 3d.   Doors open 6-30.

J. Broadbent & Co., Printers, Hudd.   **No. Early Doors.**

Things to do at Christmas in Huddersfield.

TELEPHONE No. 131.

Contractor to Her Majesty's Mails

Thomas Darwin,

STAGE COACH PROPRIETOR,

LIVERY STABLES,

FARTOWN,

HUDDERSFIELD.

ABRAHAM SWALLOW, DEIGHTON, HUDDERSFIELD,

. . HOSIER . .

And Knitter of Stockings, Socks, Cardigan Jackets, Boys' Jerseys, Ladies' and Children's Vests, and various Underclothing.

Retail Dealer in Yarns, &c.   Customers' own Yarn Knitted to Order.   Socks and Stockings Re-footed.   Dealer in Woollen Patterns for Patching and Rug Work.

John Allen Smith,

Coal and

Coke Merchant.

FURNITURE REMOVER.

Sheepridge,

Huddersfield.

MRS. TOM ODDY,

Butcher,

SHEEPRIDGE, HUDDERSFIELD.

❖❖❖❖❖

Potted Beef AND Pickled Tongue.

❖❖❖❖❖

Orders promptly attended to.